THE RE

THE NORTHERN PLAINS

INDIAN WARS

FRED BANKE

<u>The Reale Deal</u>

The Northern Plains Indian Wars

Authored -Photography and Published

by

Fred Banke

ISBN: 9798391354246

Printed in the USA

DEDICATION

This book would not be possible without the help and generosity.
of my friends in North Dakota.

I dedicate this book to Marcus Waters and the families of Jeff Hurley, Vess Hurley, Jerry Zimmerman, and Arthur Anderson.

INTRODUCTION

I first became interested in the Northern Plains Indian Wars when I researched property in North Dakota, where I was invited to metal detect artifacts. The more I researched, the more I learned about how the Indians were misled. How both parties were guilty of some horrific acts of war.

This book is designed to help understand the complexity of the Northern Plains Indian Wars. How they started, a look into the lives of military and Indian leaders, information on forts used to support the expeditions, the battles, and the massacre involved.

To accommodate the influx of immigrants to the country, the United States Government drove the Native Americans west. As the settlers moved west to farm the fertile land and prospect for gold, conflicts between them and the Indian Nations grew. The wagon trains heading west had to pass through the Indian territory. The government needed gold to finance the Civil War, which meant protecting the prospectors. As a result, treaties with the Indians were broken. The military had to define ways of making the Tribes stay on the designated reservations. Forcing them to change their way of life from nomadic and hunting buffalo to farming.

TABLE OF CONTENTS

The Buffalo

Throughout history, buffalo have been a staple to the survival of the Indians of the great plains. I think the government realized this and believed; if the buffalo became extinct, so would the plains Indians.

Buffalo would live up to 30 years, weigh up to 2,200 lbs. stand up to 6 ½ feet tall, and be up to 11 ½ feet long. Hunting them at a top speed of 36 mph could be very dangerous. Two hunting methods were used; running the herd and shooting from behind were the least risky and the least productive. Surrounding the herd, and trying not to stampede them, would allow them to be killed from all directions proving to be the most efficient. Bows and arrows were preferred until repeating rifles were available. Reloading a muzzle-loading gun while on horseback at high speed was difficult. One of the techniques used was to ride close to the right side of the buffalo, shoot the buffalo and break off to the right; this was done on specially trained horses.

There was an etiquette among the hunters, each man would hunt for their family, and each kill could be recognized by markings on his arrow. At times designated hunters would be tasked with hunting for families without the ability to hunt. There would always be a feast following the hunt, and the men would butcher the meat. The meat to be preserved was cut into thin slices to be dried or smoked over a fire. The women were tasked with processing everything else. Nothing from the buffalo would go to waste. The hides, hooves, brain, intestines, and even the tail would be used. **Horns** were used for cups, spoons, powder flasks, and headdresses. **Tanned hides** for Teepee (Teepee (Tipi)) covers, moccasins, clothing, bedding, pillows, belts, and pouches. **Raw hides** for containers, moccasin soles, shields, sheathes, bridles, saddles, bindings, lariats, and drums. **Bones** for knives, hoes, saddle trees, scrapers, and war clubs. **Hair** for padding, stuffing, ropes, and headdresses. **Bladder and stomach**, for pouches, buckets, and cups. **Tail** for whips, fly brushes, medicine switches, and water vessels. **Sinew** for thread, bowstrings, and bindings. **Brain** for tanning and **hooves** for glue. Due to the lack of firewood, **chips** were collected and used for fuel and smoking.

Edible parts include meat, marrow, tongue, liver, jerky, fat for cooking oil, intestines, and blood for pudding.

Below: **Hide** being processed and **Teepee (Tipi) cover**.

Shield

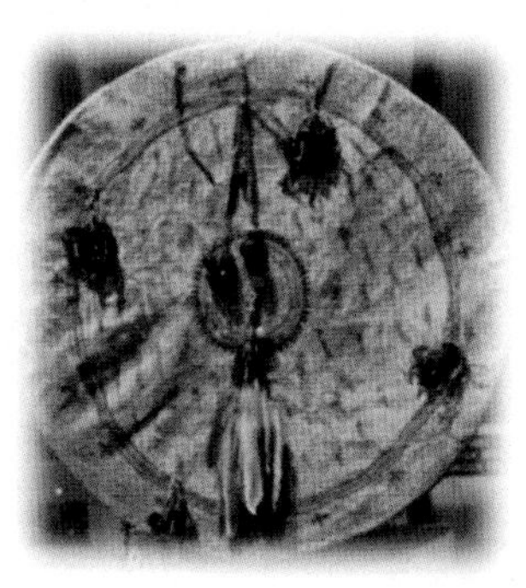

Hair-Filled Pillow

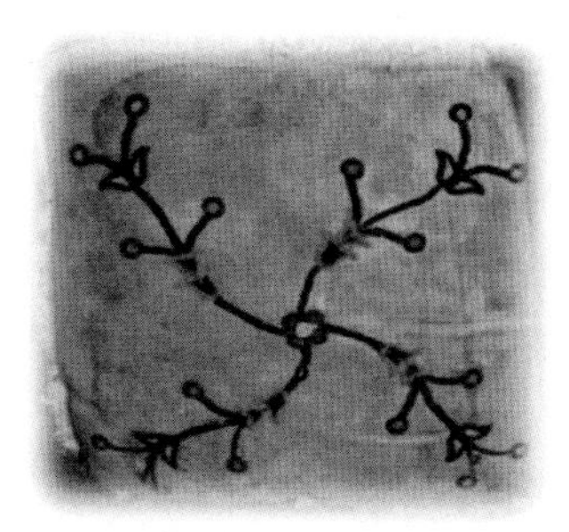

Bladder Container

Hide Purse

Horn Spoons

Powder Horn and Ammunition Pouch

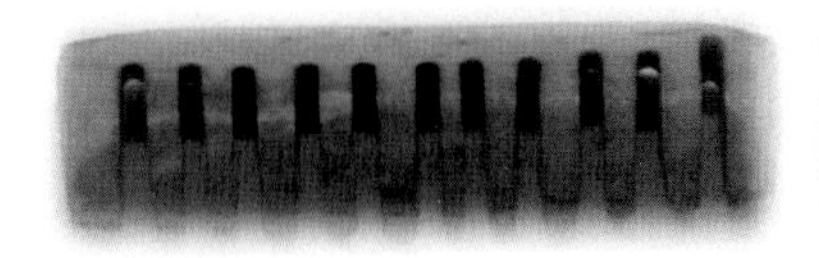

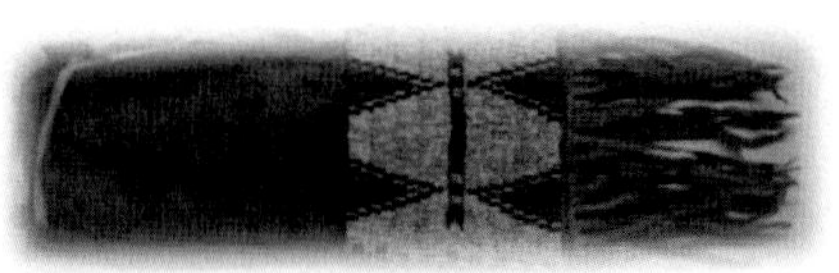

Bone Comb

Leather Pouch

Shirt

Moccasins

Bow and Shield, Harness, and Bone Paint Brushes

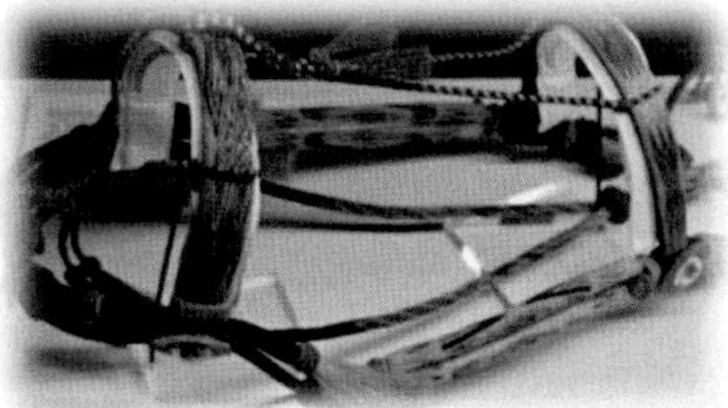

These examples of items produced from Buffalo are on display at the Akta Lakota Museum and Cultural Center, located in Chamberlain, SD.

"Akta Lakota "means "to honor the people." These words were chosen to honor the Lakota people. The museum's goal is to preserve these people's rich culture. The museum is located on the campus of St. Joseph's Indian School. The museum displays Indian artifacts, artwork, and educational items.

Examples from the meditation garden of the Akta Lakota Museum and Cultural Center

The Dakota War of 1862-Sioux Uprising

The Dakota Nation had been pressured into trading large amounts of land to the Government in a series of treaties. They were very reluctantly moved to reservations along the Minnesota River and encouraged to farm instead of the hunt as a food source.

Following a crop failure in 1861, a very harsh winter prevented the Dakota from hunting and providing meat for their survival and on the verge of dying. Tension was raised in the summer of 1862 by the US Government not providing the annual payments and food according to the treaty. Without these payments, the Dakota could not purchase food and supplies from the traders who refused to credit them. The lack of funds from the Government was due to the Civil War.

By August 1862, the tensions were very high; four Dakota hunters stole eggs from settlers, leading to five settlers' death. The following day, Little Crow, the Chief of the Mdewakanton band of Dakota, led a raid against the Lower Sioux Agency, the agency that provides the money and food according to the treaty. In the following weeks, Dakota warriors led by Little Crow, attacked, and killed hundreds of settlers, taking hundreds of mostly women and children prisoners. The response of the US Government was prolonged due to the demands of the Civil War.

In late September, the Dakota were defeated by Colonel Henry Hastings Sibly with volunteer infantry, artillery, and citizen soldiers in the Battle of Wood Lake. Little Crow and a band of 150 warriors fled the Dakota Territory to Canada. A total of 358 settlers, 77 soldiers, and 29 volunteers were lost in this war. Three days later, 269 hostages were released to Sibly's troops. 2,000 Dakota were taken into custody, of which 1,658 were not involved with the uprising; some had not only opposed the war but had helped to free hostages. The US Congress abolished the reservations, declared the treaties void, and moved the Dakota to a reservation in South Dakota and later to Nebraska.

In less than six weeks, a military commission conducted 400 trials of Dakota warriors; 303 were sentenced to death. The convictions were reviewed by President Lincoln, who approved the sentences for 39 of the men. On December 26, 1862, 38 were hung, being the largest mass execution in our history.

Punishment of the Sioux continued.

The Cast

Sully

Alfred Sully graduated from West Point in 1841. After fighting in the Mexican War, he was chief quartermaster of the U.S. troops at Monterey, California. He was accepted into the community and lived in the home of Don Manual Jimeno and his wife, Dona Augustias, daughter of one of the richest and most powerful men in California. While finding sanctuary with the Jimenos, Sully fell in love with their fifteen-year-old daughter, Manuela, and proposed. As they were Catholic and he a Protestant without a dowery, they objected, forcing the couple to elope. After several months of rejection, there was a reconciliation. Don Manual gave the couple a large tract of land and servants. Sully considered resigning from the Army and settling into a life of a California Don with a wife and a newborn son. This dream was short-lived; Manuela died of poisoned fruit, said to be from a disappointed suitor. Tragically his son died less than 3 weeks later of accidental strangulation.

In 1853, Sully left California to spend time as an Army Engineer building forts across the West (including Fort Buford), protecting the increasing number of overland travelers. This work frustrated Sully, dealing with ill-informed and inexperienced travelers.

While at Fort Pierre, Nebraska Territory, he met and married a young French-Yankton girl. She was the daughter of a powerful medicine man and chief of the "Half Breed Band."

At the beginning of the Civil War, Sully was commissioned as colonel of the 1st Minnesota Infantry. He sustained a minor wound leading his regiment at Glendale during the Peninsula campaign. Then promoted to brigadier general and led brigades in the Battle of Fredericksburg and Chancellorsville. After failing to suppress a mutiny by the 34th New York, where several companies refused to fight on the grounds, their 2-year enlistment was about to expire. Brig. General John Gibbon failed to have Sully court-martialed. He was removed from command, never to fight in the Civil War again, and sent to the Great Plains for the Indian Wars.

After going West and being an Indian fighter, Sully gained notoriety for several massacres against natives. His expeditions were directed against the Arapaho, Sioux, and Cheyenne. The most notable battle (if you can call it a battle) was at Tahkahhakuty (Kill Deer Mountain), a trading village of Yankton, Dakota, Hunkpapa Lakota, and Blackfeet. The Army destroyed 1,400 Teepee (Tipi) s; men, women, and children were killed or captured, and even dogs were ordered shot. It was described by a scout as the "perfect massacre." Some Indians were able to slip away at night through the rugged terrain, but Sully could not follow due to low supplies. Trooper casualties in this attack were few. After this massacre, he had said, "I believe I can say I gave them one of the most severe punishments that the Indians ever received." It is hard to believe he could complete this massacre knowing his connection to the Yankton, his wife being half Yankton and daughter of a chief.

Sully and troops traveled to Fort Pierre in present-day South Dakota and built Fort Sully, where they would winter.

A few years later, in 1869, he married again in Manhattan, New York, to Sophia Palmer. He continued in the Indian Wars until his death on April 27th, 1879, at Fort Vancouver, Oregon. He was buried in Laurel Hill Cemetery, Philadelphia.

Custer

George Armstrong Custer entered West Point Military Academy in July 1857; after the course was shortened due to the Civil war, he graduated in June 1861. The class started with 79 students. Due to the Civil war, 22 dropped out to join the Confederate Army, 23 due to academic reasons, and 34 graduated. Custer had one of the worst records in the academy's history, with 726 demerits; he graduated 34th of the 34 attendings.

Trained officers became in high demand during the Civil war. Custer was commissioned as a second lieutenant and assigned to the 2nd U.S. Cavalry. Always leading his men into battle setting a good example, he was recognized for his qualities as a cavalry leader. He earned numerous promotions throughout the civil war, six of which were for gallant and meritorious service in five battles and one campaign. Participating at the First Battle of Bull Run, the defenses of Washington D.C., the Peninsula Campaign, the Siege of Yorktown, and the Siege of Petersburg. Also distinguished himself at Waynesboro, Dinwiddie Court House, and Five Forks.

Promotions included; First Lieutenant, 5th Cavalry July 17th, 1862, Captain Staff, June 29th, 1862, Brigadier General, U.S. Volunteers, June 29th, 1863, Brevet Major July 3rd, 1863 (Battle of Gettysburg), Captain, 5th Cavalry May 8th, 1864, Brevet Lieutenant Colonel, May 11th, 1864 (Battle of Yellow Tavern), Brevet Colonel September 19th, 1864 (Battle of Winchester), Brevet Major General, U.S. Volunteers, October 19th, 1864 (Battle of Winchester and Fisher's Hill), Brevet Brigadier General March 13th, 1865 (The Campaign ending in the surrender of the Army of Northern Virginia). Major General U.S. Volunteer Service April 15th, 1865 and Lieutenant Colonel 7th Cavalry July 28th, 1866.

As part of the Union occupation forces, Custer was given command of the 2nd Division of Cavalry, Military of the Military Division of the Gulf

Coast. After moving to Texas, he became the Chief of Cavalry of the Department of Texas. In November 1865 Custers Division was mustered out and replaced by the U.S. 6th Cavalry Regiment. After mustering out, several members of his 2nd Wisconsin Cavalry planned to ambush Custer; he was warned the night before and escaped the attempt; the soldiers had previously considered mutiny. On February 1st, 1866, Custer was mustered out. After assisting President Johnson to build support for his policies towards the south and keeping a promise to Custer, he was appointed Lieutenant Colonel of the newly formed 7th Cavalry.

Headquartered at Fort Riley, Kansas, they would use Fort Hays as a supply base scouting Kansas and Colorado. After taking part in an expedition against the Cheyenne, Custer was arrested and suspended for leaving the post to be with his wife; he had become AWAL. Returning to his post early under the orders of Major General Sheridan, he took part in establishing Camp Supply in Indian territory. Custer then led the 7th Cavalry to attack the Cheyenne encampment of Chief Black Kettle in the Battle of Washita River. He reported killing 103 warriors, women, and children, taking 53 women and children prisoner, and shooting 875 Indian ponies. This helped move a large portion of the Southern Cheyenne onto reservations.

In 1873 Custer went to the Dakota Territory to escort a railroad survey crew. They met their first resistance from the Lakota, and one soldier and one Lakota were killed. The following year, Custer led an expedition into the Black Hills, where they discovered gold which caused a gold rush.

Custer was ordered to Washington to appear as a lead witness in a congressional hearing against the Secretary of War, William Belcamp. Apparently, he had been selling the lucrative Trading Post position for the Forts. The soldiers were charged exorbitant prices for supplies, and Custer experienced this first hand. Belcamp was impeached, Custer asked to be excused from further testimony. With the help of Brigadier General Alfred Terry, he was dismissed. President Grant intervened, and he was ordered to stay. Custer requested meetings with the President three times, only to be refused. He then gave up and took a train to Chicago, not wanting to miss the Indian campaign. Custer was arrested when he arrived in Chicago for leaving Washington without permission, causing immediate public outrage. Grant changed his mind and said Custer could lead the expedition against the Sioux but only under Terry's supervision. Grant's administration was worried if the campaign failed without Custer, Grant would be blamed.

By now, the tension between the Government, Lakota Sioux, and Cheyenne was high; immigrants continued to move westward, breaking treaty agreements and resulting in violence from both sides. When the Indians refused to allow the Government to purchase the Black Hills, Grant set a deadline of January 31st for all Lakota to return to their reservation or be considered "hostile." Custer and the 7th Cavalry left Fort Abraham Lincoln on May 17th, 1876, part of a larger Army to gather the Indians.

The spiritual leader of the Sioux nation, Sitting Bull, had gathered the Plains Indians in Montana to discuss the problems with the whites. They later moved to a camp along the Little Big Horn River in Crow country. This upset the Crow, who sided with the Army to expel the Sioux.

Custer and the 7th Cavalry would follow this trail to the Little Bighorn. On June 25th, Custers scouts identified a sizeable Indian encampment near the river. Custer had intended to attack the following day, but he decided to attack immediately as his presence was known. Custer and his men were annihilated by the Sioux and Cheyenne warriors.

Custer received a bullet wound below the heart and one to the left temple. All of the troop's bodies were scalped and mutilated in terrible ways. Custer was not; his only mutilations were an arrow projecting from his rectum. Two Indian women had shoved sewing awls in his ears to allow Custer's corpse to hear better in the afterlife. He had broken his promise to Stone Forehead. A warrior approached to take Custer's scalp but was driven away by the 2 women saying they were relatives to Custer's lover Mo-Nah-Se-Tah. In the Cheyenne culture, they were considered married.

After the battle of Washita, Custer would have her come to his tent every night and is said to have fathered her child. Some historians believe this was impossible as Custer was impotent after having syphilis at West Point.

Custer's body was buried there at the Little Big Horn and later moved to West Point Cemetery.

Much controversy remains over the disaster at Little Bighorn, Major Reno's failure to attack the south end of the village, and his retreat after only losing one soldier. This, along with Captain Benteen's tardy arrival and failure to help Custer. Some blamed Custer for his tactical errors; he refused an additional four companies from General Terry. He left the Gatling on the steamship, knowing he would face superior numbers. Before leaving camp to attack, all troops left their saber with the wagons. His decision to advance after learning he was outnumbered by so many warriors.

President Grant criticized Custer's actions and considered it a sacrifice of his troops.

Indian people emphasized Custer's role in the Government's atrocities, with land, theft, treaty violations; and the attack on Washita River where women, children, and elders were killed. Custer was following orders from Generals Sheridan and Sherman; to conduct total war on these people, even to the extent of extermination of men, women, and children. The soldiers could not pause to determine male or female or age. Custer and his men were known to have taken sexual liberties with the captured women.

Sitting Bull

Sitting Bull (Thathanka Lyotake) at birth, named Jumping Badger (Hoka Psice) and nicknamed Slow (Hunkesni) as he was said to be careful and unhurried in nature. At 14 and on a Lakota raiding party to take horses from a Crow encampment, the warriors included his father and uncle (Four Horns). He rode in the camp and killed one of the surprised Crow warriors. This display of bravery was witnessed by one of the other Lakota raiders. After returning to their own camp, his father gave a celebratory feast for his son. To mark his son's passage into manhood as a Lakota warrior. He gave his son four things; an eagle's feather to wear in his hair, a warrior's horse, a buffalo hide shield, and his name "Sitting Bull." The name in Lakota language means something like; "buffalo who set himself to watch over the herd," which simplified means "Sitting Bull." I believe his father knew he was destined to be a great leader. His father then took the name, "Jumping Bull."

Sitting Bull grew in both stature and knowledge amongst his people to become chief during the following years. His people were not involved with the Dakota War of 1862, where hundreds of settlers were killed by Dakota people trying to drive the whites away, yet they were soon to pay the price. The U.S. Army retaliated in 1863 and 1864 against Indians, and tribes not involved in the hostilities. In 1864, Brigadier General Alfred Sully arrived with 2,200 soldiers to attack a Lakota and Dakota trading village. Chiefs Sitting Bull, Gall, and Inkpaduta were there and driven out into the Badlands, where the Battle of the Badlands took place.

This enraged Sitting Bull; he did not want to be confined to a reservation. Escaping the Badlands and accompanied by 100 warriors, they ran into a wagon train where Sitting Bull led an attack on a group of soldiers tending a wagon that had overturned in a creek. Sitting Bull was shot in the left hip, which exited through the small of his back; it was not serious.

From 1865 to 1868, the leader of the Oglala Lakota, Red Cloud, fought the Army, attacking many of the forts, trying to keep control of the Powder River Country of Montana. He was supported by Sitting Bull, who made numerous attacks on Forts Berthold, Stevenson, and Buford. This uprising was known as the "Red Clouds War."

In early 1868, the government, growing weary of the conflict, met with Red Cloud, and agreed to his demands. They would abandon Forts Phil Kearny and C.F. Smith. Gall of the Hunkpapa and other Hunkpapa, Blackfeet, and Yankton Dakota representatives signed a peace treaty called the "Treaty of Fort Laramie." Sitting Bull did not sign the treaty and declared "he would not sell any part of his country." He continued his raids on Fort Buford and others in the area of upper Missouri. Sitting Bull went on to become the "Spiritual Chief of the Sioux Nation."

Sitting Bull's warriors continued their attacks on settlers, forts, and the railroad surveyors. Even when the surveyors were accompanied by troops, they were driven back. In 1874 Lt. Col. George Armstrong Custer led an expedition into the Black Hills. He discovered gold, causing a gold rush into the area. This further complicated this matter, and after failing to purchase the land from the Sioux, they instructed all Sioux to return to their reservation. Those that did not comply were labeled “hostile” and gave the Army free reign to hunt down Sitting Bull and his followers.

In 1875 at a gathering of the "Sun Dance," Northern Cheyenne, Hunkpapa, Oglala, Sans Arc, and Miniconjou attended, led by Chief Sitting Bull and Cheyenne medicine man, White Bull. Sitting Bull had a revelation, "the great spirit has given our enemies to us. We are to destroy them. We do not know who they are. They may be soldiers. White Bull then said, "no one then knew who our enemy were-of what tribe." The following year, they would learn who.

Constantly on the move, Sitting Bull's followers continued to grow to about 10,000. His leadership attracted warriors and their families, creating villages within the camp. Lt. Col Custer and his 7th Cavalry came upon Sitting Bull's camp on June 25th, 1876. Custer attacked the village, only to be eradicated; this was called "The Battle of the Little Big Horn." The Indian victory was short-lived, as, over the next year, thousands of more troops were assigned to the area.

The Lakota were pursued, forcing many to surrender and return to the reservations. Sitting Bull led his followers into Canada, where he remained for four years, causing tension between the Canadian and U.S. Governments. While there, he met and befriended an old enemy, Crowfoot, leader of the Blackfeet. He was so impressed by him, he named one of his sons after him. Hunger and desperation forced Sitting Bull to return to the United States and surrender at Fort Buford, ND. On July 19th, 1881. The following day, Crow Foot, his son, would surrender his Winchester 44 rifle in a ceremony. Speaking through an interpreter, Sitting Bull said.

"I surrender this rifle to you through my son, whom I now desire to teach in this manner that he has become friend of the Americans. I wish him to learn the habits of the whites and to be educated as their sons are educated. I wish it be remembered that I was the last man of my tribe to surrender my rifle."

On July 29th, he and his followers were transported by the steamboat, General Sherman, down the Missouri River to Fort Randall, where he was reunited with his daughter, Many Horses, living with 2,800 Lakota's that had previously surrendered. After 20 months, they were allowed to move back north to the Standing Rock Agency.

In 1884 Sitting Bull was allowed to travel with a show called the "Sitting Bull Connection," He met a young sharpshooter named Anny Oakley. He was so impressed by her accuracy with her guns, he adopted her, calling her "Little Sure Shot," the name she used throughout her career. The following year Indian Affairs agent James McLaughlin, again allowed him to leave the reservation and go on tour with "Buffalo Bill Cody's Wild West Show." He became a popular attraction and was paid $50 a week (about $1,440 today) to ride around the arena. He was not happy doing this and returned home after four months.

A Paiute Indian from Nevada visited Standing Rock, preaching the resurrection of the Natives; it was called the "Ghost Dance Movement." They would dance and chant, wearing shirts that were said to stop bullets, believing deceased relatives and the buffalo would return. Sitting Bull allowed the dancers to visit his camp but did not participate, but he was blamed as an instigator.

Fearing Sitting Bull was about to flee with the Ghost Dancers, Agent McLaughlin ordered him arrested. At 5:30 AM on December 15th, 1890, 39 reservation police and 3 volunteers surrounded his house. They knocked and entered his home where Bullhead, told him he was under arrest and led him outside. Sitting Bull and his wife made as much noise as possible to wake their people, which worked as many villagers came to the house. Bullhead ordered Sitting Bull to mount a horse, and Sitting Bull refused and was forced onto the horse. This enraged the Sioux, and Catch-the-Bear shot Bullhead, who then shot Sitting Bull in the chest. After Police officer Tomahawk then shot Sitting Bull in the head, he fell to the ground. Bullhead and six other police were killed, seven of Sitting Bulls supporters were killed.

Sitting Bull's body was taken to Fort Yates and buried. It was later exhumed by his family, brought to his birthplace near Mobridge, South Dakota; a monument stands where he was buried.

Crazy Horse

Crazy Horse was born in the center of the universe for the Oglala Sioux, the Black Hills of South Dakota. His father was Crazy Horse, an Oglala Sioux; his mother, Rattling Blanket Woman, died when he was only 4 years old. Children were not permanently named until they earned a name; he was named “Curly Hair” or "Light-Haired One. "Similar to the sacred White Buffalo, but most called him Curly.

At 12, he killed a buffalo and received his own horse. At 14, he ignored the rituals of the Sioux, riding into the prairie on a vision quest of war medicine. He fasted for 2 days and had the following vision:

During a storm, a warrior on horseback had long braided hair, a small stone behind his ear. He rode out of a lake, and the horse seemed to float and dance throughout the vision. Bullets and arrows flew around the warrior as he charged forward; neither he nor the horse were hit. A thunderstorm came over him, his people tried to hold him back, and he was struck by lightning, leaving a zigzag symbol on his cheek and white marks like hailstones on his body. The warrior told Curly that as long as he dressed modestly, his tribesmen could not touch him, and if he did not take scalps and war trophies, he would not be harmed in battle. The vision ended with a red-tailed hawk shrieking off in the distance.

His father interpreted the vision and said that the warrior would be him. Later, he dressed modestly; his war paint was lightning on his cheek and dotted white on his body, believing he would be unharmed in battle. People would become enamored by his cunning, bravery in action, and ability to overcome the enemy.

His first love, "Black Buffalo Woman," was at the age of 16; while he was out on a raid, she married a man named "No Water," but this was not the end of this love story. As time passed, he continued to pay Black Buffalo Woman attention. When No Water was out on a hunting party, they eloped. After only one night together, No Water returned and took his wife back, damaging Curley's nose and breaking his jaw. Black Buffalo Woman went on to have a light-skinned daughter, and Curly was suspected of being the father. He did marry Black Shawl, who died of tuberculosis At 17, he returned from a battle with Arapaho warriors and captured several of their horses. His father, Crazy Horse, gave him his name and took the name "Worm." Crazy Horse became a ferocious fighter and born leader; elders would consult with him when planning war parties. His first kill was a Shoshone raider who had murdered a Lakota woman washing buffalo meat along the Powder River. He fought in numerous battles between the Lakota and their enemies among the Plains tribes, the Pawnee, Blackfeet, and Arikara.

Tensions became high in the region, with the immigrants traveling through the Sioux hunting ground to the Montana goldfields.

In 1854, Lieutenant John Lawrence Grafton, 29 troopers, and an interpreter had entered a Miniconjou camp to arrest a man for stealing a cow. The cow had wandered into the camp, and someone butchered it to feed the people. The soldiers fatally shot Chief Conquering Bear. The Lakota returned fire, killing all soldiers and the civilian interpreter. In 1864, the Third Colorado Cavalry decimated the Cheyenne and Arapaho in the Sand Creek Massacre. Oglala and Miniconjou bands allied with them against the US Military. Crazy Horse was in a council at Bear Butte to bring the tribes to unity to resist the military; he told them to keep our ways and sacred land. He was present in the Battle of Platte Bridge and Battle of Red Butte in July 1865. Because of his fighting ability and generosity to the tribe, he was named an Ogle Tanka Un, Shirt Wearer, and War Leader by the Tribe. He was a War Chief of the Oglala at only 24 years old. His reputation as a warrior grew, as did his fame among the Lakota. They told accounts of him in their oral histories.

During Chief Red Clouds War in 1866-1868, Chief Crazy Horse joined the raids against the white settlements and forts in Wyoming. One such attack was at Fort Phil Kearny, After a diversionary attack on a party of woodcutters. Captain William Fetterman led a detail of 53 Infantrymen and 27 Cavalry troopers out of the Fort. Crazy Horse lured Fetterman with infantrymen by acting as if he had fallen off his horse and running next to it up the hill. The cavalry followed the 6 other decoys along Peno Head Ridge and toward Peno Creek, where the several Cheyenne women taunted the soldiers. Cheyenne leader Little Wolf and his warriors hid on the opposite side of Peno Head Ridge, blocking the return route to the fort. Warriors swept over the hill, attacking the infantry. Additional warriors hiding along the creek surrounded the soldiers. The cavalry headed back towards Fetterman, but the combined forces of 1,000, killed all of the soldiers. This was known as the Fetterman Massacre, the Army's worst defeat on the Great Plains up until that time. The Cheyenne and Lakota called it; the Battle of Hundred in the Hand.

After the treaty of Fort Laramie was signed in 1868, the Army agreed to abandon the posts along the Bozeman Trail, with Chiefs Red Cloud and Spotted Tail settling on reservations. Crazy Horse would not settle on a reservation.

In 1874 Crazy Horse learned Custer had led an expedition into the sacred Black Hills and found gold at French Creek. Prospectors and speculators swarmed into the Sioux land, ignoring the Laramie Treaty that guaranteed the land to the Lakota. To ensure the safety of the settlers, the government issued an order requiring the Sioux to stay on the Great Sioux Reservation. Along with others, Crazy Horse ignored the order, and the Army organized a campaign against them. The Lakota came together with the Cheyenne and Arapaho on the Upper Rosebud Creek in Southern Montana. General George Crook led an army of 1,300 to attack the 1,200 warriors led by Crazy Horse. Chief Crazy Horse, over the years, had become a daring military strategist adept in the art of decoying tactics. His feinting and assault techniques baffled Crook, who withdrew on June 17th. He then joined Sitting Bull and Gall at the Bighorn River in Montana.

When Custer attacked on June 25th, 1876, Crazy Horse led his warriors against Custer from the North and West, and Gall charged Custer from the South and East. Hunkpapa warriors led by Gall were the main body of the attack. Crazy Horse's tactical and leadership role in the battle leads to a flanking assault ensuring the death of Custer and his men. His courage was remembered by eyewitnesses: Water Man, an Arapaho warrior, said Crazy Horse was the bravest man he ever saw. He rode closest to the soldiers shooting at him and was never hit. Sioux battle participant Little Soldier said. The bravest fighter in the whole battle was Crazy Horse. After the battle, the Sioux encampment split up with Sitting Bull going North and Crazy Horse back to the Rosebud River. On September 10th, 2 battalions of the Third Cavalry led by Captain Ason Mills captured a Miniconjou village of 36 Teepee (Tipi's) in the Battle of Slim Butte. American Horse and family were trapped in a cave and killed. Crazy Horse attempted to rescue the camp but was unsuccessful. January 8th, 1877, the last battle was fought at the Battle of Wolf Mountain in Montana Territory. Intense harassment by the military loss of a food source (buffalo) made Crazy Horse and his followers struggle through the winter. Weakened by hunger and the cold, he decided to surrender to Fort Robinson, Nebraska, to protect his band of 3,000 followers. The time for war is over, the buffalo gone, as is our way of life. He was promised a reservation in the Powder River country (it never happened) The last Sun Dance was held in honor of Crazy Horse one year after the Battle of Little Bighorn to offer prayers for him in the future trying times ahead. Crazy Horse attended the Sun Dance as an honored guest but did not participate in the dancing. Crazy Horse lived in his village near the Red Cloud Agency. Rumors of his desire to slip away and return to his past ways of life spread throughout the Red Cloud and Spotted Tail agencies. In August 1877, officers at Fort Robinson received word that Nez Perce Chief Joseph had escaped the reservation in Idaho, fleeing North to Canada. Lieutenant Clark asked Crazy Horse and Miniconjou leader Touch the Clouds to join the Army against Chief Joseph. They objected, saying they had promised to remain at peace when they surrendered. With the fear of growing trouble at the Red Cloud agency, General George Crook was ordered to stop at Fort Robinson. Council with the agency leadership was called, then canceled when Crook was incorrectly informed.

Crazy Horse had said the night before that he intended to kill the General during the proceedings. He ordered Crazy Horse arrested, then departed, leaving the post Commander, Lieutenant Colonel Luther P. Bradley, to carry out his order. Additional troops were brought in from Fort Laramie. On September 4th, two columns moved against the village, only to find they had scattered during the night. Crazy Horse had fled to the nearby Spotted Tail agency with his wife, ill with tuberculosis. After meeting with a military official at Camp Sheridan, the adjacent military post. Crazy horse agreed to return to Fort Robinson. Upon arrival, he was arrested and taken under cover of darkness to Division headquarters, Crazy Horse was taken to the Post Guardhouse, once inside, he struggled with a guard and attempted to escape. A soldier came from behind and stabbed him in the back with a bayonet. He was taken to the Adjutants office and tended by the assistant Post surgeon. Little Big Man said that; Crazy Horse crossed over to the spirit world one last night on September 5th, 1877. The body was turned over to his elderly parents, taken to Camp Sheridan, and placed on a burial scaffold. His remains were then moved to an undisclosed location. Crazy Horse had a vision at the Sun Dance of being stabbed twice. There was never a picture of Crazy Horse. He never lost a battle and was never captured "You have two sets of eyes, one you see through, and one you see the truth through your heart."

Fort Union Trading Post

Established by the American Fur Company in 1828, near the Missouri and Yellowstone rivers The American Fur Company, owned by John Jacob Aster, built Fort Union. The construction was overseen by Kenneth McKenzie, who became the first Bourgeois (head trader).

Fort Union Trading Post was one of the most important trading posts in the upper Missouri region. The Assiniboine, Crow, Cree, Ojibway, Blackfeet, Hidatsa, Arikara, Mandan, and other friendly tribes traded at the fort.

The Indian tribes had been trading in this area for hundreds of years with the fur traders from the east, gaining the opportunity to exchange for European goods. The Indians, traded buffalo robes, beaver, fox, otters, and other skins. The fur traders offered guns, pots, knives, beads, blankets, and fabric. Nine buffalo robes would trade for a gun. Tribal customs were adhered to during the trading, giving gifts, smoking pipes, and giving speeches. This all would happen in the large trading room, with chiefs and leading warriors negotiating the trades for their tribes. Many of the traders would marry Indian women, strengthening the relationships with the tribes. As generations progressed, the offspring became traders, and these were called "Metis" due to their mixed blood descent.

As many as 25,000 buffalo hides were sold for over $100,000 in merchandise each year. At the height of trading, as many as 200 workers would be employed. Two needs were met; the buffalo robes were fashionable in the East. The reduction of the supply of buffalo would reduce the food supply for the native Indians, making them more willing to be relocated. The fort remained in business until 1867 when the need for hides was reduced.

Brig. General Alfred Sully visited Fort Union and chose the location for Fort Buford nearby. Company I, 30th Wisconsin was stationed at the fort to guard his supplies.

After being driven away from Fort Buford by artillery Sitting Bull went to Fort Union and complained to David Pease, the head trader who provided food without opening the gate. Sitting Bull swore vengeance and demanded a red shirt that he would wear when he returned to Fort Buford. He was thrown down the shirt, and Buford was notified to shoot the Indian in the red shirt. There was never a record of Sitting Bull attacking the fort in the shirt. He complained to Fort Union fur trader on another occasion, saying, "I have killed, robbed, and injured too many white men to believe in peace. I would rather die on the battlefield with my skin pierced with bullet holes."

There was a main and inner gate, allowing entry to the trading room, but controlled the access to the courtyard.

The **Bell Tower** would announce the opening and closing of the gates and the call to meals,

The Trade House East had a large reception room where the trades would occur, and a smaller space would hold the trade items. Luxury goods for the Indians included the bright military-looking jackets for the men and the beads for the women. Indian beads were made from porcupine quills dyed the various colors. The guns traded would replace the traditional bow & arrow and spears and later were used on the white settlers.

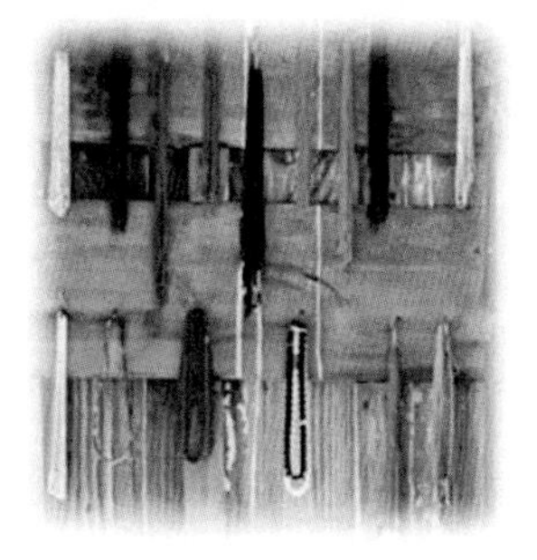

The **Trade House West** is where clerks and traders keep ledgers, inventories, and records.

Other facilities:

Storage Range, a row of shops and storerooms for trade goods, meat, and furs. **Dwelling Range**, a row of housing for employees and families. **Ice House**, an underground cellar that stored river ice lasting until August. **Blacksmith Shop** for forging and repairing ironwork and

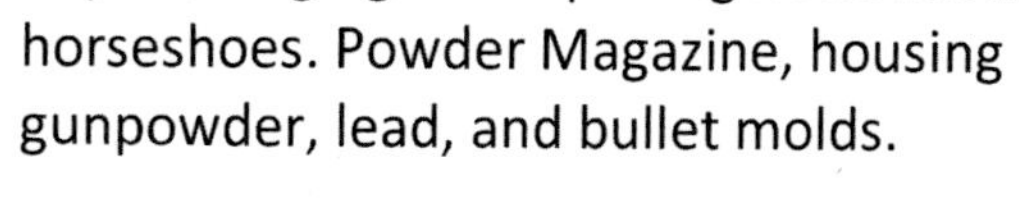

horseshoes. Powder Magazine, housing gunpowder, lead, and bullet molds.

The Bourgeois House, home of the Bourgeois, which was enlarged into a 2-story house, provides a dining room for the clerks and traders. This is now the forts Visitors Center, complete with a display room, store, and National Park Rangers to answer questions.

On display in the Bourgeois House (the welcome center) are many Indian artifacts.

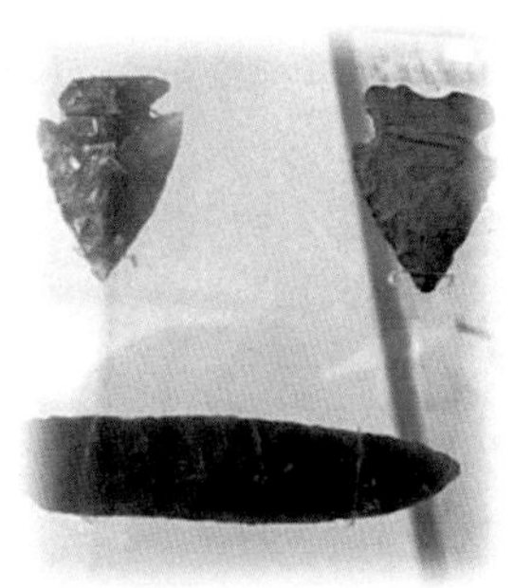

Indian toys and horseshoes from the period

Hardtack were used throughout the period while traveling.

Period clothing & personal items

An example of a Dugout canoe and stretching hides

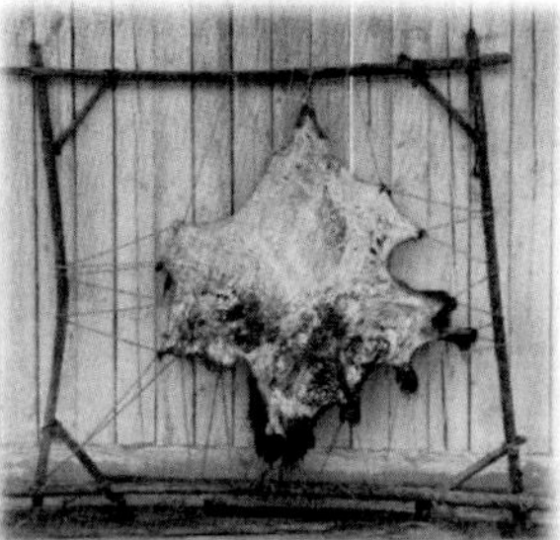

A demonstration of wooden bucket building

Moccasins

Blacksmith shop

The ***Yellow Stone*** was a steamer that would bring supplies to the fort.

The fort was rebuilt on its original footprint and is operated daily by the National Park Service. There are reenactment days, and you can often see Park Rangers dressed in period clothing. Various demonstrations take place, from metal forging to bucket building. I was impressed the most by the guy in the trading dressed in the period doing a great job of explaining the trading materials and trading history. Fort Union is located 25 miles southwest of Williston, on the Montana/North Dakota border. The fort is in the Central time zone (North Dakota), and the parking lot is in the mountain time zone (Montana). The Park operates on central time.

Fort Hays

Originally, named Fort Fletcher, Fort Hays was built as a frontier military post. Tasked with protecting military roads, US. Mail, stage, and freight lines and the construction of the Union Pacific Railroad from attacks by the Cheyenne and Arapaho Indians.

It was located at the confluence of the Big Creek and the North Fork of Big Creek. It was a low-lying area along the Big Creek southeast of current day Hays City. In the spring of 1867, it was destroyed in flood and killed nine Buffalo Soldiers and civilians. The fort was relocated close to the railroad to establish a supply depot to support other posts and the Indian wars.

In the summer of 1867, a cholera epidemic hit the area. Many people died, including a lady caring for the ill at the fort. She was buried at the foot of a hill nearby and soon became folklore as people claimed to see her ghost around the fort. She is known as the "Blue Light Lady."

Hays City was a railhead where thousands of cattle were driven north from Texas to be shipped east. It was also the major outfitting station for wagon trains heading west. It soon became one of the deadliest cities, notorious for its saloons and brothels where 37 licenses to sell liquor were issued in one two-day period. Known for its bloodshed and low value to human life.

Wild Bill Hickok was hired as Marshal to clean up the town from 1867 to 1869. He killed two soldiers, two civilians and wounded several others. He moved to Abilene to avoid the military authorities. Another character named Jim Curry killed several black men, threw them in a dry well, cut another man's throat, and threw him into a boxcar. After meeting an 18-year-old in the street and telling him to put up his hands, the kid pleaded for his life, but Curry shot him through the heart and stepped over his body.

On another occasion in 1869, the military accumulated supplies the fort could not hold; they were covered with a tarp and guarded by two watchmen. One night John Hays was on duty and relieved at midnight; he walked over to Tommy Drumm's saloon to check the time. As he was about to open the door, three soldiers from the Thirty-eighth Infantry (Buffalo Soldiers from Fort Hays) approached and one shot him dead. They had come to town to get drunk; a brothel had refused them entrance due to their condition and they destroyed a black barber's shop. The following day, the sheriff and barber went to the fort where the barber identified the three soldiers, who were arrested. After taking them to Hays City, they were locked up, only to be broken out by vigilantes. They were taken to a nearby railroad trestle and hung by their necks. The following day, they were taken back to the fort and buried.

In 1874, the Ninth Regiment of Colored Cavalry (Buffalo Soldiers) were stationed at the fort, something happened to incite them. A group decided to go to town and seek revenge for the 3 soldiers hung for killing Hays. They armed themselves to "clean out" the city. A fight broke out between the citizens of Hays City and the soldiers; six soldiers were killed and thrown into a dry well. From that day forward, the citizens of Hays City were determined to have law and order.

There is a piece of ground in a town known as "Boot Hill," the burial place for those who died of violent deaths; they were buried with their boots on. Forty-Five of these characters were buried there in "Boot Hill."

Fort Hays became one of the key Army posts of the Indian Wars; the fort reservation covered 7,500 acres. It was not an actual fortification but a frontier settlement where troops and supplies could be dispatched to support Fort Dodge and Fort Supply. During the 1868-1869 campaign against the Cheyenne and Kiowa, Maj. General Philip Sheridan, supported by Lt. Col. George Custer and the 7th Cavalry, used the fort as its headquarters. Custer would continue to operate from the fort until the 7th Cavalry was reassigned to the south.

Originally an Army scout, Wild Bill Hickok became Marshall at Hays City. Buffalo Bill Cody supplied Buffalo meat for the railroad and continued to scout for the Army. Buffalo Bill would later form a "Wild West Show," which would take Sitting Bull on tour as an attraction.

Buffalo Soldiers in the 10th Cavalry and the 38th Infantry were stationed at the fort until they moved south to fight the Indian wars and then north to Fort Buford, North Dakota.

A limestone Block House was built in 1867. It was initially intended to be a barracks; although it had rifle slots, they were never used to defend the fort. The limestone was quarried two miles to the west. When the wooden barracks were constructed, the Block House became the commanding officer's headquarters and post adjutants living quarters.

Wood was brought in by rail to complete the construction of all of the other buildings.

A stone guardhouse was built in 1872 to replace the original wooden one. It included a "non-commissioned officer of the guard" room, guard room, and a prison containing 3 separate cells. Most prisoners were there for disorderly conduct, desertion, insubordination, and even murder.

Officers Row was a series of 10 houses built between 1867 and 1870. These duplexes would house 2 officers and their families. Each had a parlor and bedroom; the dining room and kitchen were shared. Servants could be hired to help with cooking, childcare, and cleaning.

Elizabeth Custer would accompany her husband to Fort Hays from Fort Riley, where she stayed.

Behind each of the houses on "Officers Row" are the outhouses for each building.

Note: Many of the original buildings have been removed and replaced with a silhouette showing where the building existed.

Officers' tents were also supplied if no housing was available. At times, 3-4 would share quarters in a house. These were assigned by rank and seniority; if a high-ranking officer was transferred in, they would bump a lower-ranking officer out, called "cranking out." Officers and families would live in the tents on the fort grounds; some would use more than one tent, they had woodburning stoves, wooden floors, and they would furnish them. At times officers would allow their wives and children to live in the quarters while they lived in tents and would stay in the houses over the weekend. The officer tents were miserable in the blowing snow and summer heat.

The Commanding Officers House was a single-family residence containing a parlor, dining room, kitchen, and two bedrooms on the first floor. Upstairs were four bedrooms, a servant's quarters, and a storage room.

Quarters master's location was a massive complex containing; offices, non-commissioned officers' quarters, warehouse, shops, and wagon shed.

He was in charge of all equipment, transportation, supplies, animals, construction, building repairs, and post inventory.

The shops included blacksmiths, wheelwright, carpenters, and saddlers.

Laundress Quarters consisted of four wood-frame buildings known as "Sudsville" or "Laundress row." Each building housed four laundresses and their families in two 12 ft by 12 ft rooms. The laundress would wash for 15-20 soldiers paying $1 per month and extra for overcoats, pants, and bed sacks. Privates would earn $13 a month, being married to a laundress would double the households' earnings. For an enlisted man to marry, he would have to get permission from his commanding officer; it was only granted if the company had room for another laundress.

The original wood bakehouse burned down in 1875, it was in disrepair, and the oven needed constant repair. It was replaced with a stone building. All of the fort's bread was baked there, although the thought of fresh-baked bread sounds good; at the time, it was believed that the bread should sit in the open for 48 hours before eating. Fort hays bread was known to be sour and doughy. Regardless of their skills, troops were detailed to be bakers.

The forts garden was located near Officers Row. Rations during the Indian wars were terrible, encouraging all forts to plant vegetable gardens to supplement the diets, adding nutrition for the soldiers. Crops grown were lettuce, radish, green peas, string beans, corn, beets, turnips, onions, sweet potatoes, cabbage, and watermelon.

The Surgeons Quarters was a one-story, four-room, frame building. He would keep detailed records of soldiers, civilians treated, and deaths and births at the fort. The surgeon also acted as a health inspector for plants, animals, and the weather. The post-hospital was prefabricated in St Louis and shipped by rail to Fort Hays, assembled in 1867 as a 36-bed hospital. In 1870, it was expanded to 44-beds. The facility included a limestone morgue, outhouse, and hospital steward's house.

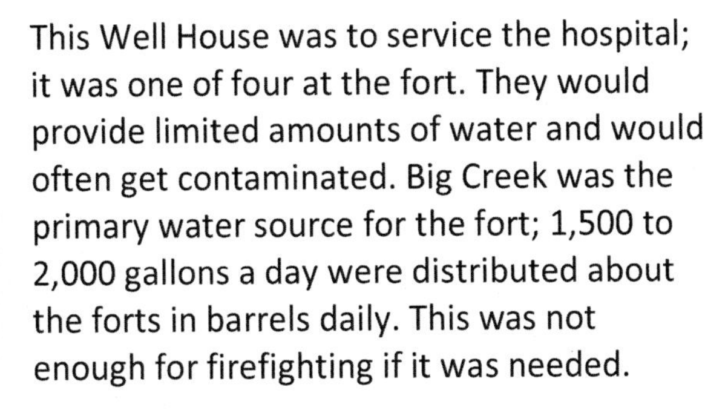

This Well House was to service the hospital; it was one of four at the fort. They would provide limited amounts of water and would often get contaminated. Big Creek was the primary water source for the fort; 1,500 to 2,000 gallons a day were distributed about the forts in barrels daily. This was not enough for firefighting if it was needed.

The Chapel was brought in from Fort Harker when it closed. The officers' wives wanted a dance hall, but Army regulations prohibited military resources to build one. The 105-foot-long Chapel arrived in 1872; 25 feet were closed off as a chapel and post-school, sparsely furnished with small benches and a pulpit. The 80-foot remaining section was used for dancing and theatricals; it was more elaborately furnished. So, the ladies got their dance hall.

The Post Traders Store included his living quarters and a store where soldiers could buy combs, tooth powder, hats, blankets, and canned food. It also had separate rooms for officers and enlisted men to buy alcohol, play cards, and billiards. It was a modern-day post exchange (PX), officers club, and non-commissioned officers club.

The Cemetery contained soldiers that died near the fort, although 25 of the 175 were civilians. In 1887, the cholera epidemic claimed 23 soldiers in one month. When the fort was abandoned in 1889, the Army planned on moving the soldiers from the Cemetery to Fort Leavenworth. The residents of Hays City delayed that the fear of moving them might trigger another cholera epidemic. They were finally moved in 1905.

In 1870, the Icehouse was built into the side of a hill. It could store up to 1,000 tons of ice hauled from Big Creek.

Guard House

The storeroom in the guardhouse. Guard at the guardhouse

The Army continued to use Fort Hays until June of 1889.

Fort Hays is now surrounded by the Fort Hays Golf Club and Kansas State University. The fort is owned and operated by The Kansas Historical Society and is open to the public.

Fort Buford

The History

Fort Buford, a State historic site near Williston, North Dakota, was built in 1866 near the confluence of the Missouri and Yellowstone rivers. It became an important supply depot for military field operations protecting immigrants moving West, arriving overland and by riverboat on the Missouri River. Although Fort Buford played an essential role in protecting the northern plains, it is remembered as where Sitting Bull surrendered in 1881.

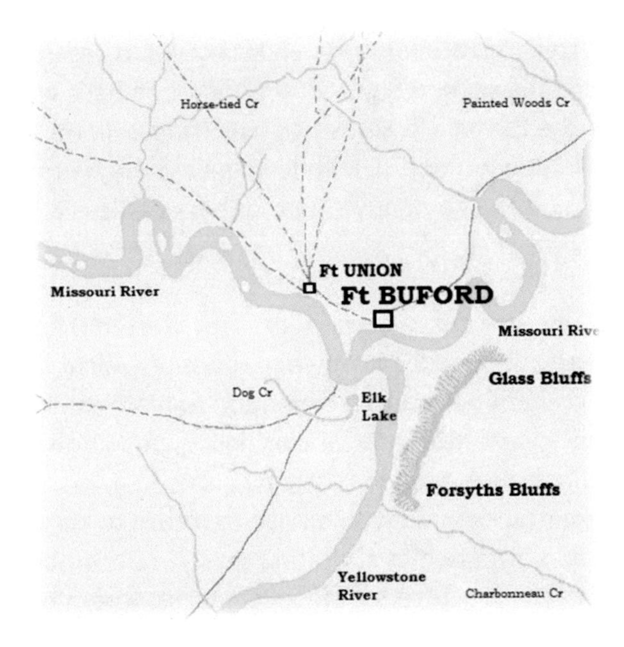

THE FORT

Buford structure was the HQ of a large military reservation 30 miles by 30 miles. Inside the reservation, The Fort was built on a 640 acre (1 square mile) area. The Fort was about 100 acres.

After failing to put down a mutiny in his ranks during the Civil War, Brigadier General Alfred H. Sully was sent West to campaign against the Sioux tribes. He was charged with finding the best location for a military fort to support these efforts.

At the time, Fort Union Trading Post was a drop-off point for supplies for General Sully's campaigns against the Sioux. Infantry was there to guard these supplies. The American Fur Company had offered the Fort Union Trading Post to the U.S. Army. As it was small in size and somewhat disrepair, Sully decided to find another location to build a fort.

As the Missouri River was an important transportation corridor, Sully surveyed the area and chose a flat, well-drained area just North of the joining of the Yellowstone and Missouri rivers and approximately two miles by land and seven miles by river from Fort Union.

This Fort would be named Fort Buford, after the late Major General John Buford, hero of Gettysburg.

Captain William G. Rankin (promoted to Lt. Colonel without a pay increase) was assigned. Captain Rankin, three officers, 80 enlisted men of Company C, 2nd Battalion, 13th Infantry, and six civilians set up camp on June 15, 1866. The second night after arrival, the base was attacked by a band of the Hunkpapa Sioux, led by Sitting Bull. He was driven off with one soldier wounded. The following day, they returned and attempted to drive off the company's herd of beef cattle. Two Sioux were killed.

More troops arrived, and the construction of the Fort started. The only materials available were adobe and cottonwood, both of which proved not to be an excellent permanent construction material. It consisted of a 360-foot-square stockade, enclosing log, and adobe buildings, constructed to house a single company garrison. Men cutting logs were often attacked and would have to return to camp, where fighting would last from two to six hours. Later, in December, at the sawmill, three civilian woodcutters were killed, Lieut. Hiram H. Ketchum, sixty men reacted, drove off the Indians, and recovered the bodies.

Attacks led by Sitting Bull continued. The Fort now besieged was cut off the garrison from the nearby Missouri River, forcing them to sink shallow wells near their quarters to obtain fresh water. The shallow well water was contaminated by the post's livestock and human waste, which caused dysentery. The Sioux repeatedly attacked and captured the post's ice house and sawmill located near the river. The attackers were finally driven off when Rankin ordered his two 12 lb. cannons to return fire.

In January 1867, Rankin received new orders that the garrison's strength would be increased by four companies. These were B, F, G & E and were to arrive that spring. Work started on a more enormous fort. The original buildings were remodeled; the Fort now measured approximately 1000 ft by 600 ft and had a 12 ft stockade on three sides. The Missouri River acted as a moat on the fourth side.

Note: Fort Buford was now the farthest northwest outpost, and many of its first troops were "galvanized" Union soldiers. They had been Confederate soldiers but were captured and forced to become Union soldiers.

Around 1870, the garrison received unexpected visitors, 150 to 200 Hidatsa and Mandan Indians from the communal settlement Like-a-Fishhook Village one hundred miles South. They were enemies of the Sioux and led by Bobtail Bull and Crow Flies High. They founded a new colony of mainly log cabins some two miles northwest of the Fort. Being close to the Fort, they realized they needed protection from the Sioux, the Military recognizing the value of its neighbors, and soon enlisted some as scouts. They later served as scouts for General Custer and several of the other units of the Army.

Construction started on an expansion in 1871-1872. This was due to the increased Indian attacks and the arrival of Colonel William B. Hazen's 6th Infantry Regiment, making it now a six-company Fort. As part of a third construction phase, the post was designed for ten companies but was ultimately built to house the six companies. Fort Union was then purchased by the U.S. Army due to the superior quality of its aged wood parts removed and used in this next expansion phase. Using this and hardwood shipped by steamer from the east coast, far impressive buildings were constructed. The Fort now covered approximately a square mile to include laundress quarters and a double row of Officers' Quarters.

The Military allowed several organizations to be on the reservation. Post Trader was one, few military forts allowed the Post Trader to be on the military reservation. Was this the source of the alcohol consumed by the soldiers at Fort Buford? Others included the Masons, Odd Fellows, and the railroad workers (the Military protected the railroad surveyors throughout the West).

The Northern Pacific Railway continued to survey West of Missouri into 1874. This provoked the Sioux, who felt they must stop the railroad at all costs. By 1875, the area became very unstable, the Military was asked to drive the Indians back to their reservations. This began the Sioux Wars, which lasted from 1876 through 1879. The Fort had become a key element in the supply routes for the campaigns, with cavalry companies sleeping in tents in the parade ground while they were being supplied. During the peak of the fighting, which included the Battle of the Little Big Horn, there would be 1,000 people.

Additional improvements at the Fort, including a sandstone powder magazine made of stone, quarried north of the Fort.

It could be one million rounds of black powder cartridges for the fort garrison and the troops passing through. By 1880, the Fort now had 90 buildings; many of the original adobe buildings deteriorated to the point they had to be replaced.

After Custer's defeat at the Battle of the Little Big Horn, Sitting Bull moved North to Canada. Resources were lacking, the need for his followers to return to their families caused the return to Dakota Territory. 187 people traveled with Sitting Bull to Fort Buford. On July 20, 1881, the great Sioux chief surrendered his Winchester .44 caliber carbine to Major D.H. Brotherton, Fort Buford's commander.

Among the regiments stationed at Fort Buford in 1885 were the Buffalo Soldiers, including the 10th Cavalry and the 25th Infantry. These soldiers were African Americans who could only serve in segregated units under the leadership of white officers. It was the Plains Indians who nicknamed the Buffalo Soldiers. Thinking their tightly black curled hair resembled the dense wooly coats of the bison. Another possible source was that they wore Bison skins as coats during the winter. The soldiers accepted this nickname proudly and were a force to be reckoned with. Buffalo soldiers had the lowest military desertion and court-martial rates of their time. The 10th, 25th, 9th Cavalry, and 24th Infantry were part of the legendary "Buffalo Soldiers" stationed in Arizona during the campaigns against the Apache.

The African American soldiers were familiar with the Masons and formed the Prince Hall Masonic Lodge, Eureka #135. Though the two Masonic lodges at Fort Buford were segregated, the African American members were recognized and respected. Social organizations allowed mingling between officers and enlisted men and between African Americans and whites. After the decommissioning of the Fort, some Buffalo Soldiers remained around the Williston area. Some went on to fight in the Spanish-American war.

An iron horse monument resides at the site of the Mason Lodge in honor of the Buffalo Soldiers of Fort Buford. The Monument itself was designed and built by Bozeman artist Jim Dolan and named “Our Work Is Done.” The statue is an athletic-looking horse with all the trappings of a Cavalry soldier. The horses head tilted toward the Southeast where the Eureka Lodge may have been, paying homage to the location. The exact location is unknown, but it is narrowed down to a spot near the river.

Original features still existing on the site include the Mason Lodge, stone powder magazine, post cemetery. A prominent officers' quarters building now houses the museum.

The Masonic Lodge

In 1889, the last of the expansions took place. The 1872 Hazen Quarters became the Field Officers Quarters, a more prominent Commanding Officer's Quarters built on the northern end of Officer's Row. A water tower was added towards the river. Due to not being able to bury the pipes deep enough, the installation of water mains to the buildings failed.

The role of the Army at Fort Buford changed to protect railroad crews and guard the Canadian border to prevent Indians and Métis from migrating into the northern plains. They would police the area against outlaws and prevent white settlers from illegally settling on Indian land. Because the Fort was no longer necessary for the Army and was in such disrepair, it was abandoned on October 1, 1895.

Today the North Dakota State Historical Society runs Fort Buford as "Fort Buford State Historic Site." Of the approximately 1 square mile, only 40 acres are currently owned by North Dakota. Inside the officers' quarters are a museum exhibit and interpretive center featuring artifacts and displays about the frontier military and Fort Buford's role. A modern restroom is located across the road from the museum.

The stone powder magazine that at one time stored as many as one million rounds.

One of the forts two cannons used to repel Indian attacks.

The remains of the guardhouse (prison) that held Indian prisoners to be transported downriver to reservations.

Prisoners of War:

While trying to escape, Yanktonai Indian Running Bear was shot and buried. Then dug up by local Assiniboins, scalped, and cut to pieces; they celebrated and danced into the night.

General Miles delivered Chief Joseph and the Nez Perce warriors from Bear Paw Mountain Battle.

Chiefs Gall and Crow King are captured and brought to Fort Buford; both were courageous in the Battle of the Little Big Horn; Gall lost his first wife there.

1,149 Sioux transferred to Standing Rock Indian Reservation and finally the surrender of Sitting Bull and almost 200 followers. It makes you wonder where they kept all of the prisoners and how they fed them all?

The Post Trader

Permanent stores were established at the forts, known as Trading Posts, and at one time, there were three at Fort Buford, located just west of the fort near the Masonic Lodge. After 1870 one store remained, operated by Leighton and Jordan, who were joined by G.M. Hedderich. With Fort Buford closing in 1895, Hedderich moved his store to Williston, North Dakota. A Hedderich store remained in business in Williston until 2017.

These Trading Posts supplied soldiers with items unavailable at the fort commissary and quartermaster stores. Available were tobacco, beer, whisky, canned fruit, shoelaces, and thread. The cost of shipping goods by riverboat up the Missouri River caused prices at the stores to be high. As the soldier's pay was low, credit would be extended to the troops and later deducted from their pay.

As long as fort regulations were adhered to, and they did not compete with the Post traders, other shops were allowed at the fort. These included a tailor, barber, hotel, and restaurant. It wasn't until the railroad arrived that more material things became available, making the fort more comfortable.

Off Duty Activities:

As Fort Buford was located away from civilization, soldiers and civilians had to entertain themselves with limited resources. Much of this time was spent consuming large amounts of alcohol and being with any available women in the area. Due to the extreme weather, climate, poor diet, hygiene, and living conditions, the low morale of the soldiers and ill health became a primary concern. Along with alcohol-related ailments, diarrhea and upper respiratory infections were common.

One of the most prevalent health problems was venereal disease. On July 4th, 1868, seven of ten men reporting sick had this disease. Among infectious diseases from 1870-1874, syphilis was ranked fourth at Fort Buford and accounted for ten percent of illnesses. Substances used to treat syphilis were mercury, arsenic, and bismuth, all considered very toxic today.

Leading by example:

A constant problem throughout the history at the Fort was the abuse of alcohol; Captain Rankin and his replacement Post Commander

Colonel Bowen, were relieved of duty for drunkenness. Rankin spent the winter under house arrest for his 52 physical confrontation with also drunken Captain Little. After repeated episodes of intoxication, Bowman was arrested and confined to quarters, where he would spend up to 15 days in a drunken state. Two soldiers acutely died of inebriation or, as we would call it now, "alcohol poisoning." So, where did they get all of this alcohol? Was it first from the Trading Post or would they get their booze from the steamships bringing supplies up the river? A small town established just South of the Fort, with a hotel and restaurant, did it come from there? Fort Buford was one of the most isolated and dangerous posts; winter blizzards and Indian attacks would keep the soldiers confined to the Fort. The winters were so bad in the Dakotas, the soldiers would create an indoor rifle range in their barracks, even with cartridges of limited power; how dangerous was that?

Other distractions:

By far, the hardest working at the Fort were the Laundresses. Each of the troops had two uniforms which meant they would be wearing one while the other was being laundered. It was no easy task, especially in the winter, as the clothes had to be hung outside to dry. (Believe me, I know; I was in the Navy Bootcamp at Great Lakes during the winter, and we had to hand wash our woolen uniforms and hang them out to dry where they would freeze within minutes.)

There was usually one Laundress for every twenty men, and their pay would be as little as two dollars per soldier per month. The Laundresses were guaranteed their wages and always first in line to collect money from the soldiers. It was deducted from their pay at the pay table before they had a chance to spend it. Some married to enlisted men, others were single with children to support. Then there was some lewd character that made additional money from the troops. These caused problems for the post surgeon as he would have to confine some of the laundresses to treat venereal diseases.

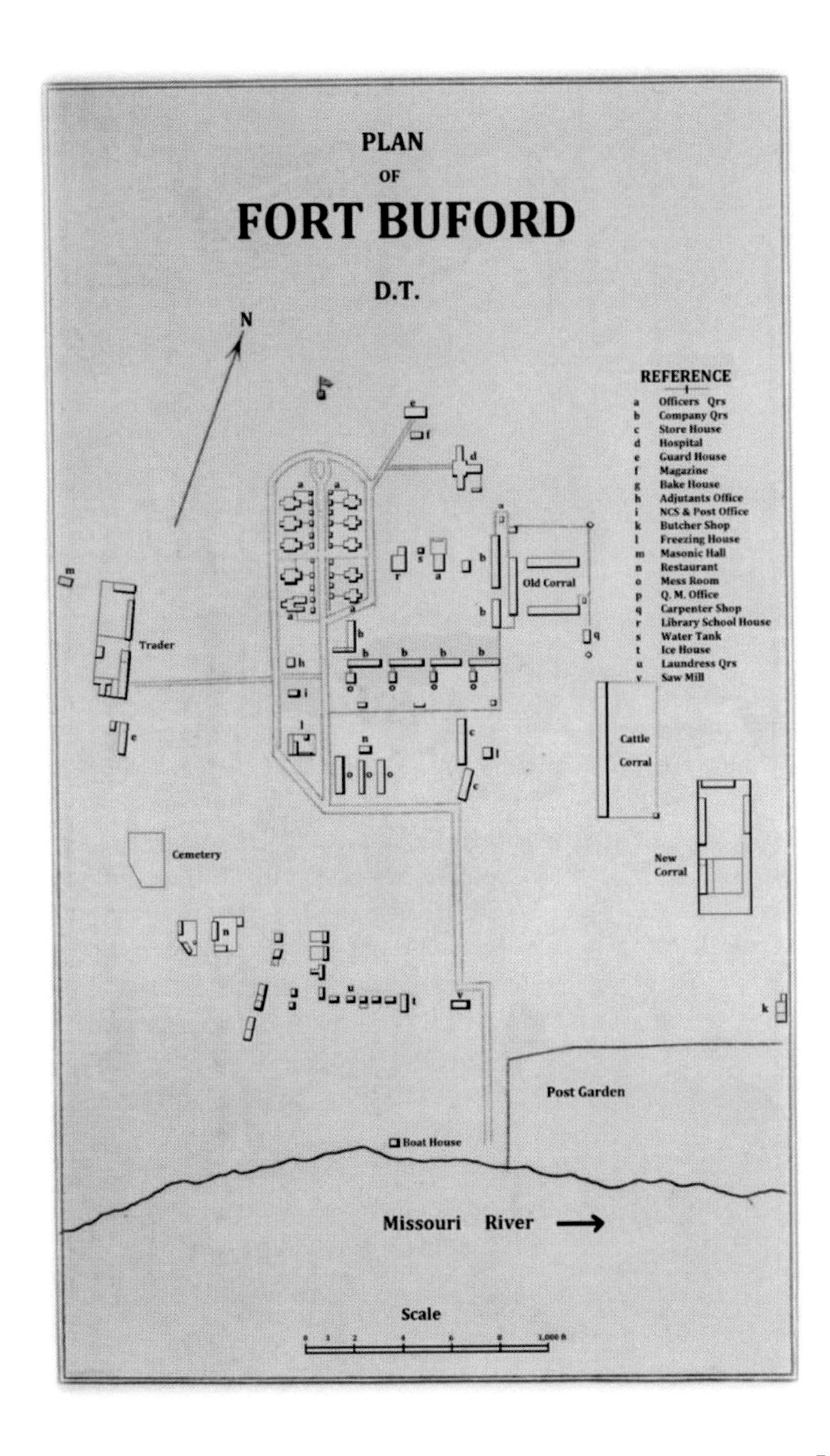
PLAN
OF
FORT BUFORD
D.T.
N
REFERENCE
a Officers Qrs
b Company Qrs
c Store House
d Hospital
e Guard House
f Magazine
g Bake House
h Adjutants Office
i NCS & Post Office
k Butcher Shop
l Freezing House
m Masonic Hall
n Restaurant
o Mess Room
p Q. M. Office
q Carpenter Shop
r Library School House
s Water Tank
t Ice House
u Laundress Qrs
v Saw Mill
Old Corral
Trader
Cattle Corral
New Corral
Cemetery
Post Garden
Boat House
Missouri River
Scale
1,000 ft

The Fort Buford Cemetery

Deaths that occurred to the Military, civilians, and Indians at Fort Buford were from, hostile Indians, murder, suicide, inebriation, and many medical issues. Bright's disease, Consumption, Cholera, Dropsy, Dysentery, Emphysema, Gastritis, Meningitis, Spinal Meningitis, Tuberculosis, Typhoid, Pertussis, Pneumonia, Phthisis and Rheumatism.

During the Buffalo Soldiers stay, a tragedy of murder/suicide occurred. Corporal John Hartwell was murdered, shot by Private Basil Williams without provocation, both from 'C' Company of the 25th Infantry. Private Williams was placed in the guardhouse following the shooting on July 17th 1894. A civilian court found Basil Williams guilty of murder. He was taken to Cass County Jail to await transfer to prison. During this time, Private Williams had taken a leather belt, placed one end around his neck and tied the other to steel, slumped down into a sitting position and found dead.

Other Buffalo Soldiers to die at Fort Burford include.

Hostile Indians caused many injuries and deaths at Fort Buford. On August 10, 1869, two miles from the fort, a party of over 100 Hunkpapa Indians attacked 4 civilians on a hay wagon. Adam Jones, Joseph Araldo, James MacLane, and Peter Dugan were killed. All were scalped, mutilated and Jones was found with 13 arrows in his body.

On May 14, 1868, 10 miles from camp, a hay wagon was attacked by Indians; 2 unarmed citizens were killed; they had left their weapons behind as things were quiet. Roach and a Negro named Tom were found the next day, beaten, mutilated, scalped, and pinned to the ground with 27 barbed arrows.

On August 20, 1868, 3 soldiers Henry Henderson, Max Lehman, and George Beals, were killed and 3 wounded while guarding 250 cattle just south of the fort.

Others were killed by hostile Indians. Blue Horn was an Assiniboine scout killed while guarding cattle. William Lee was hunting near the fort with three others when they were attacked. The Indians were driven off by the cattle guards. Theon Aldridge was attacked by 200 Indians; he killed 5 Indians before his gun was jammed; he then used his Winchester as a club to fight and was hacked to death. Red Shirt the Hunkpapa Chief said; I never saw one fight so well or die so bravely as that boy at the mouth of the Yellowstone.

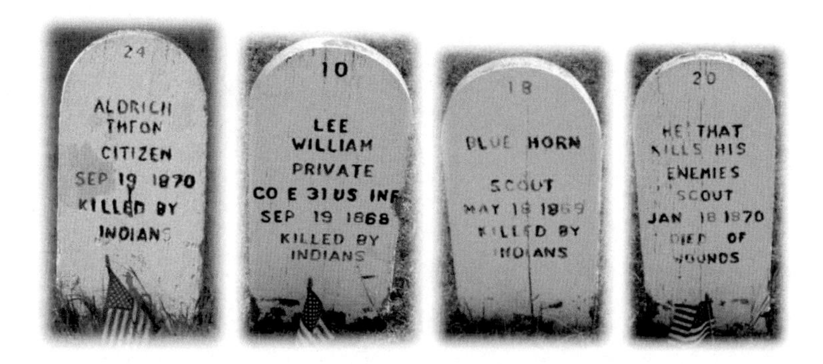

On January 18, 1870, an Indian scout, *He That Kills His Enemies*, died of a quarrel with a fellow scout by an arrow wound penetrating his pelvis and abdomen.

Some were murdered; on October 17, 1885, George Fleury, an Indian interpreter, was killed by Private Charles Wood. The latter was turned over to the civil authorities at Bismarck for trial. On December 13, 1878, Edward Shaffer was shot in the abdomen while in his bunk at the barracks by Private John Smith.

Although some Indians at the fort were indeed murdered, records do not show the circumstances; the reason for death on the headstones say killed or poisoned.

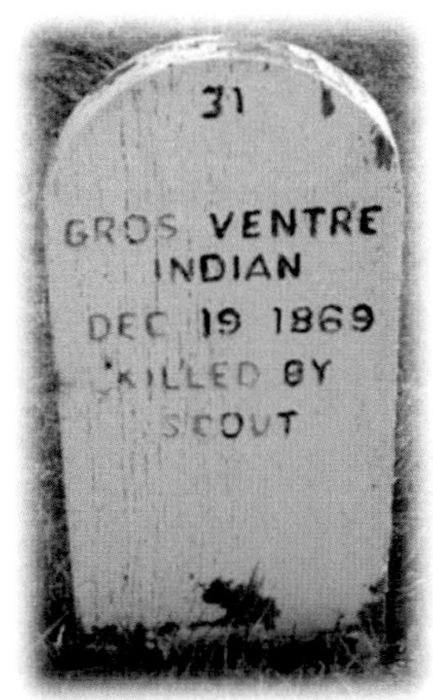

Death by Suicide; Charles McAllister shot himself through the heart; he had an imaginary disease of the brain. John Potter shot himself through the head with a Springfield 45 cal. Rifle. It was determined he was standing as the ball had passed through the roof, and small pieces of skull were found on the ceiling and on the bed, brain spattered the walls. Found on his back with a handkerchief tied to the trigger of his rifle and around his foot.

Other deaths: Bartholomew Norman of Tipperary, Ireland, died in his bunk of inebriation. There was a lot of drunkenness the previous night, and the source of the alcohol was unknown (probably the trading post). Coonrod Aquilla was shot twice in the abdomen while leading an escort for the Paymaster with the payroll traveling to Fort Buford. Seven road agents (outlaws) attacked and were driven off. Jeremiah Burrows was accidentally shot through the left foot and bled to death while on watch at midnight. A strong wind was blowing, and the shot was not heard. Louis Kramer disappeared on August 6, 1878, and was found drowned in the Missouri River; it was determined violence could have been inflicted before his death.

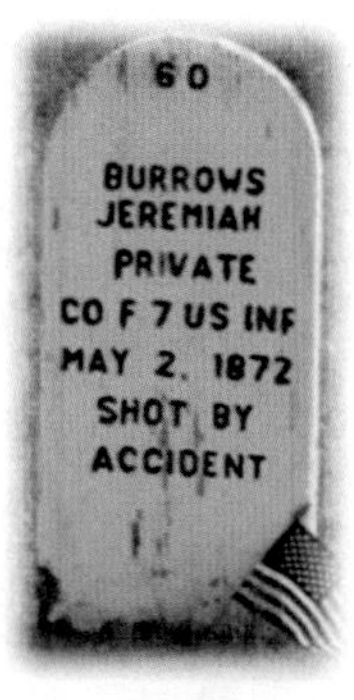

Others who died from the disease.

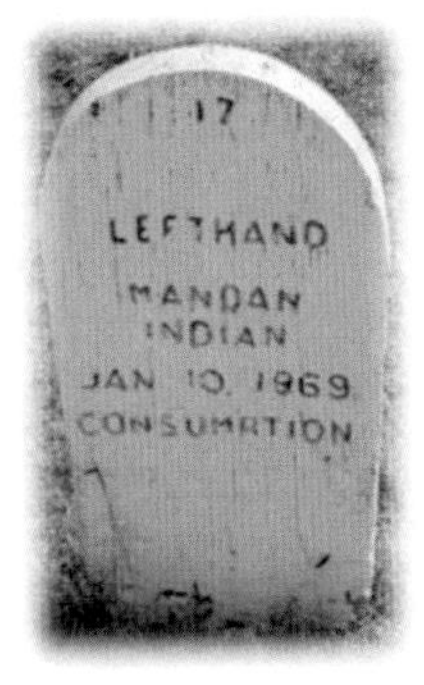

Supplies had to be brought up the river between the spring and summer. This included construction materials, food, and clothing. Mail moved up and down the river but was carried overland during the winter. The steamboats that took supplies to Fort Buford and returned with hides and furs were very large. (Photo: public domain National Archives Archaeological Site [Public domain], via Wikimedia Commons)

Woodcutters would make a living during the summer months by supplying firewood for the steamboats; this was called "wood hawking." They would leave piles of wood along the river for the boat to stop and collect; in turn, the captain would leave money in this spot for the woodsmen. It was a principle of trust; the woodsmen would rely on the captain's honesty as he knew the captain would not want to stop along the river to harvest their own wood. The captain would depend on the woodcutter to supply aged wood that was not green and hard to burn. They would often provide meat for the fort and hay during the summer and trap during the winter. Living remotely along the river made them an easy target for the hostile Indians.

The illustration below shows the rivers now compared to the river flow from 1893.

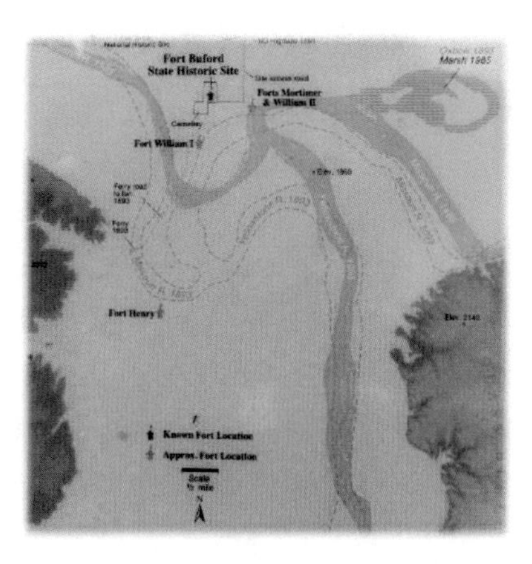

The illustration below shows Fort Buford in its current configuration.

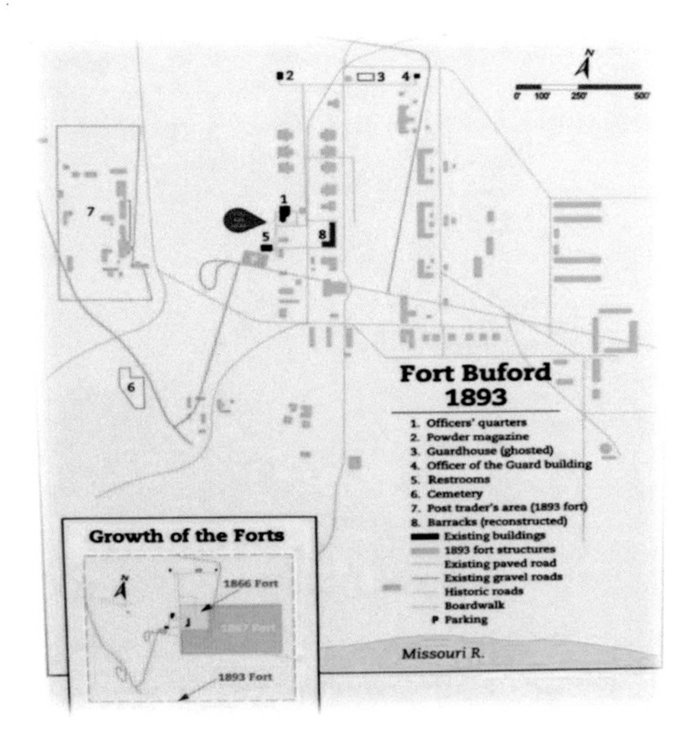

Displays inside the fort include examples of things used in everyday life and a Sitting Bull exhibit. Others can be viewed at the Confluence Center at the river.

Fort Abraham Lincoln

Formerly, Fort McKeen, Fort Abraham Lincoln is located at the site of the deserted Mandan On-a-Slant (Miti O-pa-e-resh) Indian village.

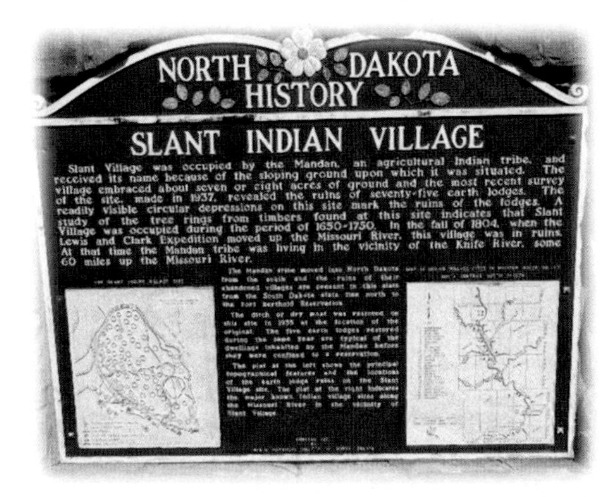

This Mandan name came due to its sloping location plain towards the confluence of the Missouri and Heart Rivers.

The fort has several Mandan and military items on display.

A Model of the Mandan Village

The village consisted of 85 earth lodges and had a population of 1500. It was one of nine Mandan villages with 10,000 to 15,000.

Different from most Northern Plains Indians, they lived in permanent homes called earth lodges. The Mandan people existed on men hunting and fishing. At the same time, women tended to crop, gathered berries, processed meat, and hides, and made baskets and pottery. Due to this diversity, the village became a trading center for the nomadic tribes who would trade skins for Mandan goods.

The women were also tasked with building the earth lodges, which consisted of a frame of cottonwood logs covered with layers of willow branches, grass, and earth.

These walls would protect the families from the cold in the winter. An opening in the center at the top would allow smoke from the fire to escape and provide sunlight to the dark interior. Each lodge would provide shelter for 10-15 family members, storage for food supplies, and protection for animals.

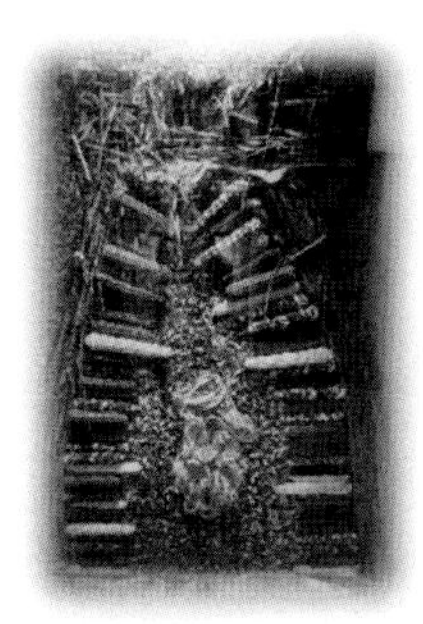

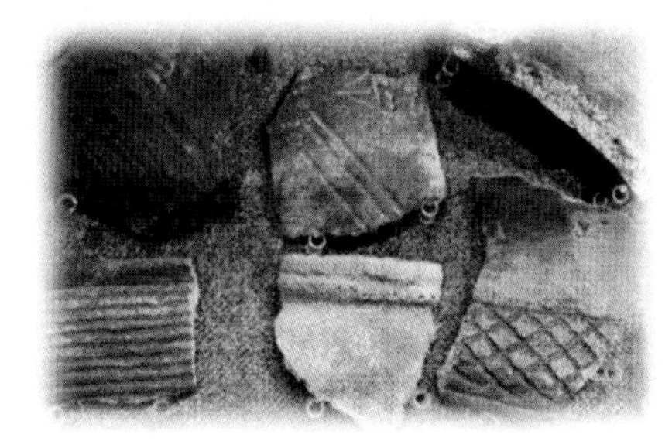

Existing at this site for 200 years, in 1781, a smallpox epidemic almost eliminated the Mandan people. The remaining people followed the Missouri river north to join the Hidatsa along the Knife River. In 1804, Lewis and Clark discovered the village deserted and in advanced decay. Six reconstructed lodges, including a large Council lodge, exist today as an insight to the Mandan people.

Almost 100 years after the Mandan moved away from the village, in 1872, a US Infantry post named Fort McKeen was established near the site of the Mandan village. The location was chosen for easy access to supply by steamers on the Missouri River. A few months later, it was renamed Fort Abraham Lincoln and was to become one of the largest and most important forts of the Northern Plains. In 1873 congress authorized the addition of a cavalry post which was completed the same year. By the following year, the forts soldiers consisted of three companies of the 6th and 17th Infantries, including Buffalo Soldiers of the 6th. They were joined by six companies of the 7th Cavalry, which complemented the fort with 650 soldiers. First to command Fort Abraham Lincoln was Lt. Colonel George Armstrong Custer, who served there from 1873 until his death at the Battle of Little Big Horn in 1876.

The fort consisted of 78 permanent structures. Barracks for nine companies, seven officer's quarters, six cavalry stables, a post office, a granary, a telegraph office, and a guardhouse. Other buildings included a storehouse, bakery, hospital, laundress quarters, scout's quarters, and a house for George and his wife, Libbie Custer.

Stables for the 7th Cavalry

In 1891, the fort was abandoned, and in 1895, a new Fort Lincoln was built on the river near Bismarck. At the original fort, the commanding officer's quarters (Custers House), Central Barracks, Granary, Commissary, and stables were all reconstructed and exist today. Cornerstones are in place to show where other buildings once stood.

Custers last residence

Whitestone Hill

In 1863, under the direction of General John Pope, two expeditions were dispatched into the Dakota Territory to dispense of the hostile Sioux Indians. A large force commanded by General Sibley, and another by General Alfred Sully, with the plan of crushing the Indians between them. Sully's troops numbered 2,000, Cavalry from the 6th Iowa and 2nd Nebraska and artillery from the 7th Iowa with four twelve-pound guns. The 2nd Nebraska was made up of volunteers recruited to protect their homelands and motivated by a soldier named Pvt. Henson Wiseman who had lost his wife and five children killed in their home in an Indian raid. The 6th Iowa were also volunteers. They were scheduled to head East and join the Union troops in the Civil war; they were diverted to Sully's command in the Indian wars. Three significant factors delayed the expedition: the late arrival of the 2nd Nebraska, Sully not assuming command until June 1st, and the shallow level of the Missouri river. The river was so low steamboats supplying the expedition had trouble navigating the river, often getting stuck on sandbars. These delays infuriated General Pope, who relayed this to Sully, and General-in-Chief Henry W. Halleck. After leaving Sioux City, the expedition headed North up the Missouri River, with lousy weather further hampering its advance. Due to bad weather, at one time, it rained for an hour, then it started to hail the size of pigeon eggs, and they had frost the following day.

June 22nd: Departed Sioux City to Fort Randall.

July 10th: Arrived at Fort Randall and the Crow Creek Agency.

July 31st: They finally left the Agency and headed to Fort Pierre.

August 12th: At the Old American Fur Company, Sully received orders to leave behind between 60 and 70, sick and disabled.

August 13th: Two of the sick die, and Sully's expedition heads further North up Missouri.

August 21st: Sully led the expedition East at the mouth of the Little Cheyenne River and Northeast toward Devils Lake. Traveling with only 23 days of rations, he only planned a brief diversion.

August 25th: Large herds of thousands of buffalo were reported by scouts. The soldiers, not experienced at hunting buffalo, managed to shoot several.

August 26th: The hunt continued and then halted after Lt. Stewart of Co E accidentally shot his own horse. Orders were given, and they could not hunt more buffalo until the return trip.

August 27th: Scouts located two Santee squaws and a papoose, who said their tribe was hunting at Beaver Creek. The tribe was not found.

August 28th: At the outlet of Long Lake, signs of a large number of Indians were found, along with an old crippled Indian named Keg. His feet had been frozen the previous winter. The others had taken his horse, leaving him to die. He was friendly and helpful, saying that the Indians had fought Sibley weeks earlier, and returned to the Missouri river. They attacked a Mackinaw boat, killing 21 men, 3 women, and 8 children and sinking the ship. The men from the boat had returned fire, killing 81 Indians and wounding more. Keg also said that most Indians had gone to the head of Long Lake. They were in a region known as the Coteau. This time of year, the Indians would camp there near the tributaries of the James River. The coteau is an uneven terrain with small hills and ravines. Numerous spring-fed lakes keep the grass fresh, attracting an abundance of buffalo, with the lakes and streams full of fish. Here they would prepare their winter supplies of food before going West to the Missouri river, where the wood supply was plentiful for the winter.

September 3rd: They were about 85 miles from the Missouri River and reached a lake. Nearby on the plains, they found numerous remains of freshly killed buffalo and signs of Indians and their lodge pole trails heading to their favorite spot. Scouting parties were sent out daily, returning to the camp at night to report their findings. On this day, 300 men of the 6th Iowa Cavalry, led by Major Albert E. House, left the encampment as the scouting party. They were accompanied by two scouts, mixed blood, named Frank LaFrambois and an Indian called Crazy Dog. They traveled to the South, stopping each hour for the horses' to graze, with LaFrambois 5 miles ahead and Crazy dog halfway splitting the distance. In the afternoon, LaFrambois came upon a small Indian camp of about 20 teepees. They returned to inform House and the troops barely 2 miles away. The troops were told to prepare their weapons, and they galloped towards the Indian camp, carefully keeping them in the valleys where they could not be seen. As they closed on the camp, they realized it was much larger, and when two officers returned from a closer look, they estimated 300 to 600 lodges. Estimates of the quantity of Indians were about 3,500, of which 1,000, could have been warriors. LaFrambois and two soldiers were sent back to Sully to report the situation and request reinforcements. Meanwhile, the Indians had discovered the Scouting party as it approached. Two companies were sent left, and after their return, another company right, reporting the strength of the defenses. The young warriors were eager to fight, but the elders insisted they wait. Indian Chiefs approached with a white flag to attempt to negotiate, offering to surrender some of their Chiefs. House demanded they all give up as he did not know who was entitled to speak for the encampment. This was abruptly rejected by the Indians. By now, three hours had passed, and House's troops were stalling for time until the reinforcements could arrive. The soldiers were ordered not to fire their weapons under any circumstances, standing in front of their horses with guns ready and occasionally changing positions to distract the Indians. Meanwhile, LaFrambois had reached Sully, and the bugle was sounded. The troops prepared their horses that had been grazing and got into formation. Leaving a small detachment to guard the camp, they were told to break down the tents and circle the wagons. Sully led his troops at a gallop towards the Indian village, it was about ten miles, and they covered it in about an hour. Several horses stumbled, throwing their riders along the way. Sully approached the camp from the West, 2nd Nebraska on his right, 6th Iowa on the left, and 7th Iowa with artillery in the center. After seeing Sully's forces approach, the Indians prepared their departure. The older Indians and the squaws were tasked with taking down the teepees, loading them on the tent poles behind the ponies, and packs were pulled behind their dogs. The younger warriors were starting to retreat towards the James River. When Sully arrived and saw the Indians leaving, he ordered Colonel Furnas and the 2nd Nebraska forward as fast as possible to assist Major House. Colonel Wilson. Part of the 6th Iowa Cavalry was dispatched to the North side of the settlement. With troops and the battery, Sully charged through the camp's center. Sully's troops gathered up a group of 120 Indians. Among them were Chiefs Little Soldier, Big Head, and members of the "Medicine Bear's Band." Left behind were the dogs and ponies all packed up ready to travel. No one seemed to be coordinating among the Army, and communication was poor, to say the least. Indians have fled, scattering about the area. Chased down by the Cavalry, a large group had taken shelter in a ravine a half mile from the village. Colonel Furnas approached the valley and had his troops form a battle line. Intending to await orders from Sully, but due to it being evening and losing light, he decided to attack. Furnas ordered his men to move into two lines, forming about a 120-degree angle, and moved forward. Now, within 400 yards, they dismounted and proceeded on foot for another 100 yards. Here the troops were ordered to open fire with their Enfield rifles inflicting casualties among the Indians.

Meanwhile, Major House and the Third battalion of the 6th Iowa arrived at the ravine, forming a battle line. After seeing the 2nd Nebraska on his left flank preparing to fight on foot, he ordered his troops to advance. They were immediately fired on by the warriors and returned fire. Next to arrive was Colonel David Wilson and the First battalion of the 6th Iowa, who formed a line opposite the 2nd Nebraska. Now confusion was caused by Wilson. He led his men into battle with empty guns and was separated from the First Battalion. His horse was shot from beneath him, and he soon found himself among the Third Battalion.

Sully had the Indian prisoners guarded and placed his troops and the battery on small hills surrounding the camp, holding the Second battalion of the 6th Iowa in reserve. At the ravine, the shooting continued for 30 minutes while they continued to lose light. The confusion and the ongoing battle made the horses of the 6th Iowa very difficult to control and unmanageable. The Warriors took advantage of this and could escape during the darkness of night. Furnas was now convinced while mistaking his men for Indians, House's troops were firing on his men. He ordered his Cavalry to retreat away from the ravine allowing Indians to escape. As the surrounding soldiers camped for the night, they were called to lay on their arms and be prepared. Not much sleep was taken that night. With the fear of the warriors in the night, heavy picket lines were ordered to guard the horses. The howling of the dogs, the squaws squalling, mourning their dead would keep them awake. It was also time for the soldiers to gather their dead and wounded.

September 4th: As morning came, it was only then they could see the extent of the damage to the Indian camp. Some teepees were still standing, others were destroyed, and others had been taken down and loaded with ponies. Dead soldiers, warriors, squaws, and some severely wounded children of all ages were missing their parents. The children were gathered and turned over to the Indian prisoners for care. Dead horses and dogs lay all around, Live ones wandering all over the countryside, with the dogs howling and trying to find their masters. 600 to 700 soldiers were involved in the battle. Of the early reports 18 were dead and 38 wounded. The Indians reported a loss of 200 and 156 captured. The loss could only be estimated as warrior bodies were collected in the dark and removed.

Sully ordered the camp destroyed, and it would take a party of 100 men to complete this in 2 days. An estimate of dried buffalo meat destroyed was 400,000 to 500,000 pounds, representing one thousand buffalos killed. Teepees, buffalo hides, food, and equipment were all burned. The melted fat ran down the valley like a stream. Anything that could not be burned, like hatchets and copper cooking vessels, was thrown into the lake. While destroying the teepees, an Indian jumped out and shot two soldiers with arrows before he could be killed.

September 5th: Troopers were tasked with burying their dead. Once covered, the Indian's property was placed on the graves and burned to protect the last resting place of the soldiers. Troops were sent out to locate the fleeing Indians. Lt. Charles Hall led one scouting party of 27 men. They found 300 warriors several miles from the camp. In this conflict, 2 soldiers were killed, and the remainder hastily retreated.

Sully had believed he had dealt the Indian camp at Whitestone Hill "one of the most severe punishments that the Indians had ever received." This severe defeat of the Indians did not come from the battle. It came from the destruction of all the winter food and belongings lost. This is how in several battles with the Indians, he would deal with them, taking away their provisions.

September 6th: Sully led his troops away from Whitestone Hill and marched towards Fort Pierre.

September 11th: After traveling 130 miles, they reached the mouth of the Little Cheyenne River and found the Steamboat they had requested. They placed all the wounded on the Steamboat and as many empty wagons as they could carry. The return to Fort Pierre was difficult. The grass had little for the livestock to eat.

Orders were given to slaughter anything that could not keep up. He did not want to leave anything useful to the enemy.

On Memorial Day 1910: 4,000 people attend a Dedication of the Whitestone Battlefield Monument.

The original graves of the soldiers were on a knoll away from the monument. The gravestones of the soldiers surround the monument-on-Monument Hill.

The only memorial to the Indians that died here, is the small plaque. It reads "In memory of the Sioux Indians that died on this battlefield September 3-5, 1863. In defense of their home and hunting ground."

Improvements were completed to the park, museum and picnic facilities, and a stone getaway.

July 18th, 1963: A 2-day Centennial Celebration, with 6,000 attending on Saturday. There was a parade, Indian ceremonial dances, and a rodeo. By Sunday, there were 20,000.
The park's size is 68 acres and now includes campgrounds.

November 9th, 2009: The artifacts in the museum were taken, and the building burnt down and later rebuilt.

The Whitestone Hill Battlefield Historical Society continues to manage the property.

Battle of Killdeer Mountain

In 1863, most of the Sioux had been pushed west of the Missouri River to create a safer environment for the white settlers. Yet, in the spring of 1864, four settlers were killed by Sioux raiders.

Recently discovered goldfields in Montana and Idaho were essential to the Government to support the Civil War. Miners and supplies would be shipped up the Missouri River by steamboat. Travel had to pass through Sioux territory; this became the lifeline for the gold miners. For these reasons, an actual military campaign was waged against the Sioux. In 1863, General Sully received orders to establish several forts along the Missouri River and in the eastern Dakotas.

Sully had two Brigades, the first with 1,700 men would follow the Missouri River from Sioux City, Iowa. Sioux warriors killed one soldier and wounded another; three Sioux were caught, killed, and decapitated. This journey was supported by 15 steamboats with additional soldiers and civilians. The other Brigade consisting of 1,550 men traveled overland from Fort Ridgely, Minnesota. The two

Brigades met on June 29th and established Fort Rice on the Missouri River in North Dakota, which steamboat could supply.

Sully reluctantly agreed to escort 200 miners and their families; this would aggravate him as his scouts had informed him of a large Sioux trading camp northwest. The scouts reported between 1,500 and 1,800 Teepee (Tipi) s, and Scully anticipated 5,000 to 6,000 warriors. The Sioux are Lakota from the Hunkpapa, including Chiefs Sitting Bull and Gall), Sihasapa, Miniconjou, and Sans Arc tribes, with some Yanktonais and Santees. They were armed with bow and arrows, short-range muskets, and shotguns and later claimed there were only 1,600 warriors.

Note: Many tribes had not been hostile before this Battle, and this attack was one of many reprisals against the Sioux.

After leaving soldiers at Fort Rice to protect the wagon train, Sully set forth with 2,200 men, two artillery batteries, and eight cannons. After 16 days of travel, his scouts encountered 30 Sioux warriors. One scout was wounded. The warriors escaped warning the settlement of Sully's presence. Sully was then informed of the location of the Sioux encampment 10 miles ahead at Killdeer Mountain on the edge of the Badlands. Behind the camp were steep impassable ravines and rugged hills, making it unlikely for a cavalry charge to succeed. He had the soldiers dismount with one soldier holding four horses. They formed a square of men one mile and a quarter on each side with the artillery, transport wagons, ambulances, command staff, and the horses protected in the center. They advanced on foot with Sioux on the hilltops and in groups surrounding them on horseback, exchanging insults at long distances.

The first shot fired was at an Indian named Long Dog carrying a war club. He gestured wildly, appeared one half a mile in front of the advancing column, and was ordered shot. There is no record of if he was actually hit. The Sioux mounted attacks at the flanks seeking weak spots. A thrust at Sully's rear was broken up by artillery shells that killed several. The cavalry mounted their horses and formed a counterattack supported by artillery, scattering the Indians. The cannons now on a hill overlooking the village began to destroy the town. Shelling the Indians in the trees behind and to the side of the village, driving them into the open. Realizing there was no chance of repelling the attack, the Indians defended their families as they fled to the rugged terrain at the rear. Sully advanced to near the village. As darkness fell, he halted his men for the night but continued with the village's destruction with the artillery. The Sioux fled, abandoning the Teepee (Tipi) s and all of their belongings, including food and buffalo hides for the winter. Sully's loss for the day was 3 killed and 10 wounded; he estimated 100-150 Sioux dead.

The following day, Sully ordered 700 men to destroy the encampment, and all left behind. In all, 1,400 Teepee (Tipi) s were burned along with tons of dried buffalo meat packed in skins. Everything was destroyed, including dried berries, buffalo robes, tanned buffalo, and elk, riding saddles, dray poles for horses and dogs, household utensils. A few Sioux left behind, including children, were killed by the Winnebago scouts. Close to 3,000 dogs were shot, and no prisoners were taken.

Some Sioux remained in the area and waved a white flag and tried to talk but were fired on by the soldiers; they finally fled. But that night, two of Sully's picket guards were killed and one wounded by the Indian party. Sully continued his pursuit of the Sioux into the Badlands.

Note: The survivors of the Battle had just a short time to replenish their supplies for the winter. The Battle did solidify the disdain for the military, especially the Lakota and Sitting Bull, that had nothing to do with the US-Dakota War of 1862.

Killdeer Mountain Battlefield is a State Historic Site, protected by the State Historical Society of North Dakota. It is located 8.5 miles northwest of Killdeer, North Dakota (in the middle of nowhere). It is in a beautiful setting, surrounded by private land, and features a sandstone monument, flagpole, and headstones to honor the soldiers killed in the cavalry charge.

A beautiful setting for a trading village

The memorial is surrounded by private property.

Fort Dilts

By now, the Dakota and Lakota Sioux were enraged by the defeats to Generals Sibley and Sully.

On July 12, 1864, six wagons headed west to seek their fortune in the Montana goldfields. Joshua and Fanny Kelly, with Fanny's 7-year-old niece Mary Hurley, two hired men, Andy, and Franklin, had recently joined the wagon train. As they crossed Little Box Elder Creek, 200 Oglala warriors approached. The group gave them several items, including Joshua's prized horse, the requested gifts, and they seemed friendly. Looking content, the warriors tried to lead them into a rocky glen; when the travelers resisted this, they insisted they feed the warriors. As the emigrants prepared to camp, the warriors opened fire on them, killing Franklin, Noah Taylor, and Sharp, a minister. Seriously wounded but escaping were William Larimer and Gardner Wakefield. After looting the wagons, the warriors departed, taking Fanny, Sarah Lorimer, her son Frank, and Mary Hurley. That night, Fanny helped Sarah, Frank, and Mary escape with the Lorimer's getting entirely away. Joshua Kelly, in a search party, found Mary scalped with three arrows in her back.

Just days following this event, a wagon train comprising of 97 wagons, 170 men, women, and children departed Fort Ridgely, Minnesota, 700 miles to the east. The expedition was led by Captain James Fisk of the Quartermasters Corp, who had made the journey on the northern route to the goldfields twice before and both times stopping at **Fort Buford**.

As they reached Fort Wadsworth, near Minnesota's western border, Fisk asked Major John Clowney for an escort as far as Fort Rice. He was to join General Sully's expedition and was given 50 men led by Lieutenant Henry Philips.

Upon arrival at Fort Rice in August, he discovered general Sully had left without him. To make things worse, he escorted a competitor's wagon train. Fisk's plan was to travel with Sully as far as the Yellowstone River; from there, Fisk felt safe as they had passed through the Sioux territory. He first tried to order Philips to travel with them. This was declined as Philips had orders to return immediately to Fort Wadsworth.

Fisk then requested an escort from Colonel Daniel Dill, the commanding officer of Fort Rice. His first request was denied, but Dill agreed to provide an escort after Fisk plead his case. Sully had left behind several men to recover from sickness and injuries from the recent battles. Dill asked for 50 volunteers but could only provide 45, the horses available were not in much better shape than the soldiers. These troops were led by Second Lieutenant Dewitt Smith, who was waiting for the outcome of a court-martial against him. Smith's second in command was Sergeant Willoughby Wells, who had just arrived from downriver on a steamboat full of supplies. Fisk had obtained a 12-pounder cannon with a limited amount of powder. The wagon train headed west on August 23 only to lose 5 of the volunteers who decided to return to Fort Rice the first night.

Fisk had decided to discover a new trail that was shorter and would save him time. Previous expeditions had taken him north past Fort Buford at the confluence of the Missouri and Yellowstone Rivers. He followed Sully's trail for about 80 miles, where Sully had turned north, Fisk turned due west traveling between the Black Hills and the Little Missouri River to the north. They would travel 6 days and rest on Sunday, giving a break for the travelers and the oxen and mules pulling the wagons.

On September 2, one of the wagons tipped over crossing a creek; Fisk ordered the wagon train to continue. Leaving behind to assist was a second wagon with its driver and 12 men as a rearguard with orders to upright the wagon and rejoin the wagon train.

The wagons and rearguard were soon attacked by 100 Hunkpapa Sioux with Sitting Bull and Gall. Corporal Williamson fought off 2 warriors that had struck him with clubs and stabbed him. Sitting Bull then rode up and shot him in the back with an arrow. Williamson turned and shot Sitting Bull in the hip with his pistol, managed to mount his horse, and returned to the wagon train to warn Fisk and later died of his wounds. The warriors killed the remaining guard and drivers at the wagons.

Sergeant Wells led his men back to protect the wagons at the rear; a scout and former Army corporal Jefferson Dilts was already on his way to help the rear guard. He shot 6 warriors. As he turned to retreat, he was shot in the back with 3 arrows. Dilts died of his wounds 16 days later. Wells and his men fought off the warriors after 2 hours to find the wagons had been stripped of new carbines, ammunition, liquor, canned goods, and silverware. The drivers and soldiers' bodies were recovered for later burial.

The Indians continued to harass the wagon train as it traveled west; finding a place to defend themselves in an area between two ridges, they made camp for the night. There was a violent storm that night; they could not take time to bury the dead, and wolves had been attracted by the scent.

September 3, they continued west, the Sioux resumed long-distance harassment firing on them with the new carbines. Fortunately, they were not very accurate with them. They did manage to shoot a few oxen and horses during the nine miles the immigrants were able to travel. Seeing the warriors had gathered a large group for the attack, the soldiers fired on them with a cannon and kept their distance. That night at camp was quiet without attack.

The following morning, some group left strychnine-laced hardtack for the Indians; this was without Fisk's knowledge and thoughts of the

Minnesota massacres. It is unknown how many died of hardtack; some believed more had been killed from that than from bullets.

The Sioux increased their attacks; Smith believed they prepared for a mass attack and looked for a defensive position. After only a few miles, they found a spot with water. They circled the wagons unhitching the livestock and gathering them in the center of the circle of wagons. One Sioux leader came a little too close to the camp; he was shot and killed, causing the others to retreat but within sight.

The number of warriors had now increased to 300 and surrounded them, with Fisk realizing he could not go any further. That night during a storm, Lieutenant Smith and 14 of his men volunteered to break through the Indian lines and ride back to Fort Rice for help. They muffled the horse hooves and were able to sneak past the Sioux, who did not realize the escape until morning when they saw the tracks. A large group gave chase believing they could cut off the soldiers before reaching the fort.

Realizing they had to fortify their camp, the travelers hitched oxen to plows and plowed large areas of sod. This was used to build a 2 foot thick by 6 foot high wall around the wagons with rifle pits and places to shoot from. This fortification was named Fort Dilts after the scout Jefferson Dilts.

On September 5, three Warriors approached the camp carrying a white flag and planted it between the groups. Once these riders had returned to the leading group, Fisk sent men to investigate and found a message wedged in a forked stick. The message demanded the wagon train leave the Sioux territory immediately, leaving behind wagons loaded with goods. The message also said that Fanny Kelly had written the note and was held captive by the Sioux. Would they please rescue her? The Oglala had traded Kelly to the Hunkpapa, and although some of the Hunkpapa could speak English, none could write it. They watched her closely as she wrote the note counting her words, but Fanny combined words to inform them of her capture. Not trusting the note, Fisk wrote back, telling Fanny to show herself. This she did by standing on top of a bluff where she could be seen with a spyglass. Fisk understood the risk she took and negotiated for two days for her release, which included giving them a wagonload of goods. The Sioux's demands were too high, and there was no guarantee the Indians would free Fanny. Meanwhile, Smith and his men wandered off the trail but later found it; the chasing warriors had passed them but never found them. Believing that the soldiers had reached the fort, the Indians returned to the leading group to continue harassing the wagon train. Smith and his men had reached Fort Rice in three days of hard riding. General Sully had returned to Fort Rice and was mad that Fisk would leave with a small escort. He ordered Colonel Dill to assemble a 900-man rescue expedition. Dill arrived at Fort Dilts on September 20. By this time, the Sioux had tired of the harassing wagon train and moved on to hunt buffalo. Fisk requested an escort through the territory, and Dill told the immigrants they could travel with him back to Fort Rice or continue on their own. All returned to Fort Rice with Dill, Fisk would lead another expedition to the goldfields in 1866. As news traveled about Fanny Kelly, the military let it be known to friendly Sioux that gifts would be awarded for the safe return of Kelly. Three months after the Fort Dilts attack on December 12, 1864, Sioux came to Fort Sully with Fanny Kelly. Kelly feared it was a scam to take over the fort and sent a message with Jumping Bear, a trusted friend to Major Alfred House, Fort Sully's commander.

More than 1,000 Sioux arrived with their captives; Major House only allowed 10 Chiefs into the fort with Fanny Kelly.

Fort Dilts is now Fort Dilts Historic Site; located eight miles northwest of Rhame, N.D. It has a site marker made of petrified wood by a local artisan and has a plaque depicting the wagon train within the fort. It also has gravestones for the soldiers and civilians that died there.

Battle of the Little Bighorn

The Treaty of Fort Laramie created a large reservation in the western half of South Dakota. The tribes at the time would travel and follow the herds of buffalo; the problem; they would be in conflict with other Indians, settlers, and the new railroads. The U.S. Government wanted them to give up this nomadic life and settle on the Reservation, where they would be subsidized for this. This was called The Great Sioux Reservation. I know this sounds very familiar to what happened in Minnesota previously and caused the US-Dakota War of 1862. Never the less several Lakota leaders signed the Treaty. Still, Sitting Bull, Crazy Horse, and other bands of warriors rejected it. They would wander free to hunt, bringing them in conflict with enemy tribes and settlers beyond the treaty borders.

By 1874, tension was escalating, and Lt. Colonel George Armstrong Custer was ordered to explore the Black Hills area within the Reservation's boundaries. He was to map, note natural resources, and locate a suitable spot for a military post. Traveling with Custer were geologists who discovered gold, and word soon got out. This caused a gold rush, an invasion that was a violation of the Treaty. All the government could do was negotiate again with the Lakota and try to buy the Black Hills area. The Lakota rejected the offer, resulting in a deadline given in the winter of 1875, requiring all Sioux to be on the Reservation by January 31, 1876. As there was no response from the Lakota, the problem was given to the military to resolve

The Indians were now considered "hostile" and forced back onto the Great Sioux Reservation. General Philip Sheridan devised a campaign, which proceeded in March of 1876. Colonel John Gibbon left Fort Ellis, Montana, with 450 cavalries and infantry. In late May, 1,000 cavalries and infantry set out from Fort Fetterman, Wyoming, commanded by General George Crook. Before this, General Alfred Terry departed **Fort Abraham Lincoln**, North Dakota, with 879 infantry and Cavalry. The 7th Cavalry was led by Lt. Col. George Armstrong Custer. The strategy was any of these three forces should deal with as many as 800 to 1,500 warriors. The problem was; communications between the three forces were challenging and slow. The Sioux were constantly on the move; no one could predict how long they would be in one place and where they would go next in search of food and water.

Large numbers of tribes would gather in early summer for the annual sun dance ceremony. This year it was near Lame Deer, Montana.

Sitting Bull had a vision of soldiers falling upside down into his village. It prophesized there was soon to be a great victory for his people.

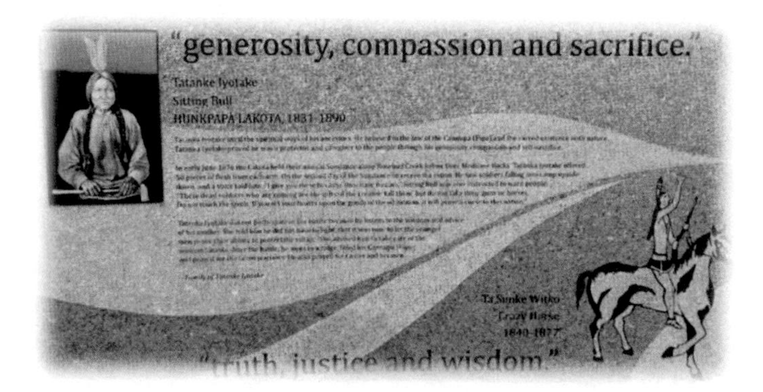

On June 22, General Terry sent Custer and the 7th Cavalry to approach the Indian camp from the east and the south. This prevented the Lakota and Cheyenne from escaping, with Terry and Colonel Gibbon coming from the north.

Custer made camp on June 24, now 25 miles east of the Indian encampment, the attack planned for June 25th or 26th. His scouts sent ahead, reported the camp was west, somewhere near to the Little Big Horn River. He ordered a night march following the trail the Indians had taken through the Little Bighorn Valley. By early morning on the 25th, they were near the Wolf Mountains, barely 12 miles from the Indian village.

The same morning, the Indian camp was full of rumors of soldiers on the other side of the Wolf Mountains to the east. Few paid much attention as there were so many of them. A Lakota named Low Dog had said, "I don't think anyone would attack as strong as we are." Estimates of the village totaled 8,000, with 1,500-18,000 warriors.

Custer's original plan was to conceal his regiment in the Wolf Mountains on the 25th, allowing his scouts time to locate the Indian encampment. He then planned to march through the night to make an early morning attack on the 26th. The scouts reported back, Custer's presence was already known by the Sioux warriors. Knowing he had already lost the element of surprise and not wanting to go into the rugged terrain, he decided to advance. The scouts changed from their military clothes to their Indian dresses. Bloody Knife, Custer's favorite scout from the Fort Buford area, was quoted as saying, **"I will not see you (sun) go down behind the mountains tonight. I am going home today, not in the way we came, but in spirit, home to my people."**

Custer ordered Captain Frederick Benteen to take the pack train and 125 men to scout the southwest, take on any Indians he encountered, and notify Custer. Major Marcus Reno, his 140 men, and the Arikara scouts were to advance to the village and "pitch into anything" they run into. With his 210 men, Custer was still out of view of the village; they were still out of view of the encampment. The scouts reported the village was scattering.

They had started this march 12 miles from the Indian village and had marched about 13 miles that night.

Reno crossed the river two miles south of the village and advanced along the river towards it. The warriors quickly gathered to stop the assault; Reno dismounted his men to form a skirmish line and fired on the Indians. Mounted warriors pushed their attack toward his left flank. For better protection, Reno retreated towards a stand of trees along the river. Reno's scout was next to him in the woods was shot in the head, his blood splattering on Reno's face. At this time, he panics and orders his men to mount, then not to mount, then to mount again. They retreat a second time, with some men not getting the word and dying there in the woods. Reno's men are fleeing for the bluffs east of the river, with the warriors shooting them at close range or dragging them to the ground. His command, now in disarray, crossed the river struggling up the steep bluffs to try and regroup to the east.

Finding no evidence of Indians, Benteen had moved back to the south. Arriving in time to meet Reno's survivors. Benteen had received a message from Custer saying, "Come on. Big Village. Be Quick. P.S. Bring Packs." Captain Weir's D Company moved north to assist Custer; heavy gunfire was heard downstream. On a high area one and a half miles from Reno's position, now called Weir Point, they saw clouds of dust and gun smoke covering the battlefield. The warriors were now heading their way in large numbers, forcing the men to retreat to Reno Hill. There they remained under siege until the evening of the 26th.

Custer had ridden north along the bluffs until he reached Medicine Tail Coulee, the natural entrance to the village. From here, it is hard to determine what happened. Still, from Indian accounts and archeological finds with the location of the bodies, historians have pieced together Custers movements.

After skirmishes at Medicine Tail Ford, at the river, Custers troops regrouped on Calhoun Hill. They moved north along Battle Ridge, while the warriors that had driven Reno into retreat now moved towards Custer. From here, it becomes a little sketchy. Companies C and L on the southern end of the ridge were overwhelmed after putting up a good fight. Company I, met the same fate on the east side. Survivors moved to the hill on the east side of the ridge. Company E was overcome while driving warriors from a deep ravine. Company F tried to hold off the warriors on the flats below before retreating up the Last Stand Hill. They had to fight their way up the hill through the Indians. 41 men were surrounded on the hill; they shot their horses using them as cover. They had run out of ammunition; some attempted to escape but were overcome by the overwhelming firepower. Any remaining wounded were shot by the warriors.

The bodies were all stripped of clothing, scalped, and mutilated, including Custer's brother Tom. Custer was found shot in the head and chest, with an arrow strategically placed protruding from his anus. Custer was known as "Long Hair" to the Indians; his only mutilation was his ears augured out. Caused due to a meeting with Stone Forehead, Keeper of the Sacred Arrows, after the Washita Battle in 1869.

Custer had sat with Stone Forehead and promised, **"I will never harm a Cheyenne again. I will never point my gun at a Cheyenne again. I will never kill another Cheyenne."** Stone Forehead poured the ashes of the peace pipe on the heel of Custer's boot and spoke. **"If you break your promise, you and your soldiers will go to dust like this. If you are acting treacherously towards us, sometime you and your whole command will be killed."**

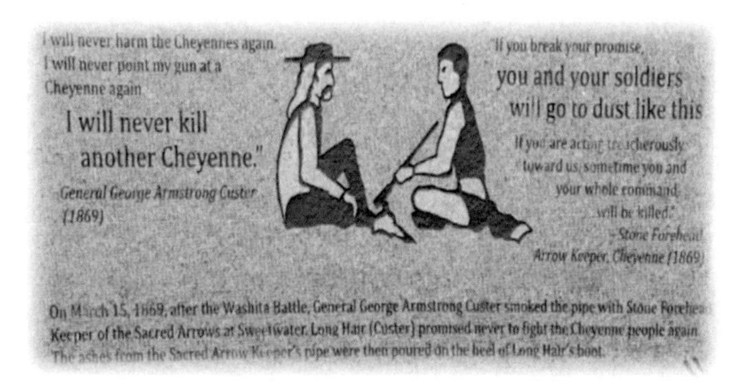

Sitting Bull had not taken part in the battle; he had decided to leave it to the younger warriors. The following day, forces of Terry and Gibbon arrived at the grounds where the Indian village had stood. The remaining defeated 7th Cavalry had now been rescued. Their Indian scouts had found the remains of the troops on the Last Stand Hill. The bodies of Custer and his men were buried in shallow graves near where they fell. The Indians had removed their 60 to 100 dead and lay in Teepee (Tipi)'s and on scaffolds on hillsides. In 1877 the remains of 11 officers and 2 civilians were transferred to cemeteries in the east. Custer's remains were moved to the U.S. Military Academy at West Point, N.Y.

In 1881 bodies of the rest of command were buried in a mass grave at the base of the Memorial. The memorials bear the names of all of the soldiers, scouts, and civilians killed in the battle.

In 1890 the Army placed 289 headstone markers where each of Custer's men fell.

Farrier Vincent Charles, a civilian, died near Last Stand Hill, where there is also a marker and graveyard for the horses of the 7th Cavalry.

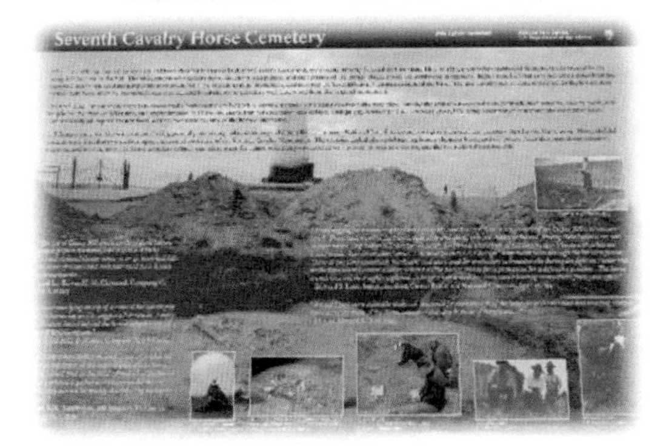

In 1919 the National Park Service erected red granite markers at each known position throughout the battlefield, where the Cheyenne and Lakota had been a casualty.

National Park Service operates the Little Bighorn Battlefield National Monument. There is a graveyard where many soldiers and civilians from the Indian wars are placed.

These are printed trail guides are available that explain the numerous trails and areas.

Last Stand Hill

The Indian Village

The-Reno Benteen Defence Area

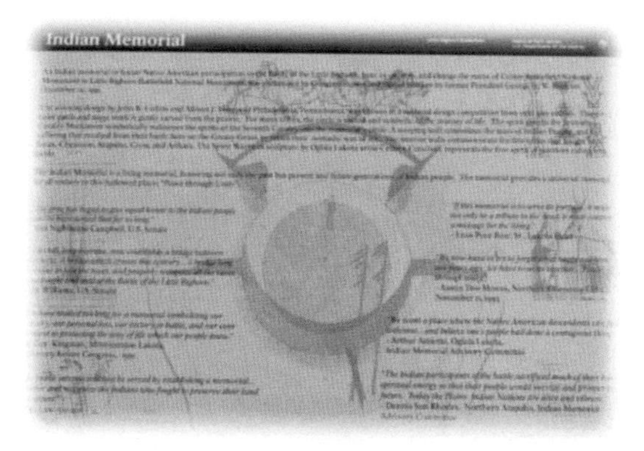

Most impressive to me, was the **Indian Memorial**, which tells the story of the tribes that took part and the stories from their Chiefs from their memories.

The Spirt Warriors sculpture by Oglala Lakota artist Collen Cutschall, representing the free spirt of the warriors as they ride into battle.

ARAPAHO (Blue Sky People) CHEYENNE (The people like us) Words of Young Two Moons: ***" It was a hot clear day and no wind. There was a great dust from the fighting, but no storm after the battle."***

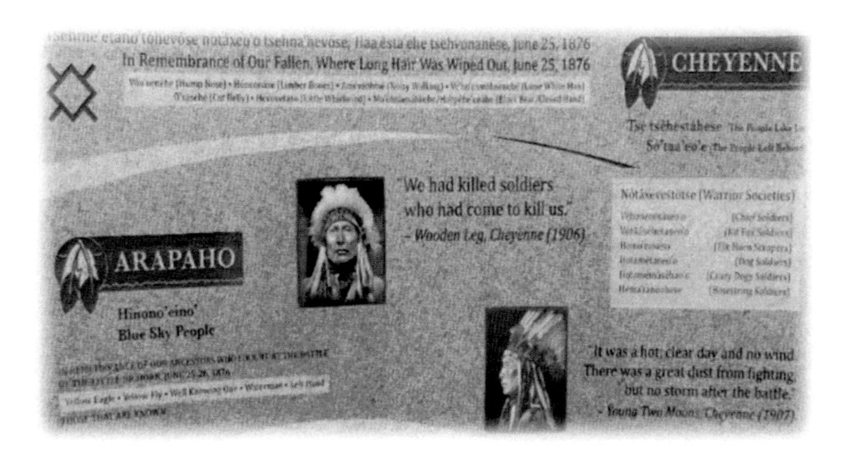

APSAALOOKE (Children of the Beaked Bird) Words of Red Wing *: **"A scout is like a lone wolf, that must be looking, looking, looking all the time."***

OYATE (We are allied Dakota-Lakota-Nakota) ***'Follow me"*** The first command spoken by the Lakota War Leaders.

Words of Enos Poor Bear Sr. ***"Power through Unity"***

The words of Brave Wolf ***"I have been in many hard fights, but never seen such brave men."***

The Words of Crazy *horse* ***"We did not ask you white men to come here. The Great Spirit gave us the country as a home. You had yours. We did not interfere with you. We do not want your civilization."***

The Celebration, the words of Gall ***"That night the Lakota men, women and children lighted many fires and danced; their hearts were glad for the Great Spirit had given them a great victory."***

The hatchet has been buried. General Edward Godfrey and White Bull shake hands. The words of Godfrey: ***"The hatchet has been with the Red race, the symbol of war. We now unite in the ceremony of burying the hatchet, holding it in covenant of our common ctizenship and everlasting peace,"***

The 1948 Gathering of the Nine Surviving Warriors.

Sitting bull had warned his people "not to take possessions from the dead soldiers." Although all of the soldiers' bodies were stripped and badly mutilated, it can't be explained where the personal and military effects treasure trove was. It is believed that there is a large cache of items hidden in a cave within a few days' travel of Little Big Horn. Today, people are still searching the area for this hidden treasure.

The Visitor Center store has a great selection of books and items regarding the Little Bighorn Battle. Volunteers do an exceptional job of giving you an insight into what took place.

Wounded Knee Massacre

I chose to call this conflict a massacre, not a battle; nearly 300 men, women, and children were killed. They could have been killed in action, but they weren't. It was the way they were hunted down, and annihilated with no regard. For their bravery that day, 20 soldiers received the Medal of Honor. You can draw your own conclusions. This massacre and the following days became the end of the Indian wars.

As discussed in this book, Wovoka, the founder of the Ghost Dance Religion, believed; the whites would disappear from the native lands, and Buffalo would return along with ghosts of their ancestors. Everything would return to normal as before the whites had taken over their land. The dance was a slow, silent shuffle and to a single drum beat; unique shirts were worn that they believed would protect them from the soldier's bullets, yes, bulletproof. The area settlers that had taken over their land were concerned, worried that the growing amount of Ghost Dancers would promote violence against them. They voiced concerns to the government, and the Army was now ordered to return the Sioux to their reservation.

After the killing of Sitting Bull by a soldier on December 15, 1890, and the conflict that followed, and fearing reprisals, Spotted Elk led his band and 38 Hunkpapa away from the reservation on December 23. Followed by another 200 Hunkpapa, they moved towards the Pine Ridge reservation and the protection of Red Cloud.

A fact to remember; they received nothing for their land. They were coerced into giving the whites the land and promised ample support and provisions, which were cut to two-thirds of the rations. The crops they grew in their new way of life were failures for 2 years, leaving many in starvation. The government had failed them again.

By **December 28, 1890**, Spotted Elk had 350 followers journeying toward the Pine Ridge Agency, established in 1879 as the reservations Bureau of Indian Affairs administrative center. It was also the military headquarters for the U.S. Army for the Winter of 1890-1891. They were intercepted by Major Samuel Whitside and a detachment of the 7th Cavalry southwest of Porcupine Butte. The orders were to disarm them and escort them to the reservation. A scout had discouraged them from trying to disarm them immediately, as it was bound to lead to violence. The Indians were escorted the 5 miles to Wounded Knee creek, where they then made camp for the night. That evening, the remainder of the 7th Cavalry, under Colonel James Forsyth, arrived with four Hotchkiss, rapid-fire mountain guns. This now brought the force of the Army to 500 and of the Lakota, 230 men, with 130 women and children.

Early on **December 29, 1890**, Forsyth ordered the surrender of the Indian weapons, and the 350 would then be taken to awaiting trains. It was bitter cold with snow on the prairie camp, and the Indians were wrapped in a blanket to stay warm. While searching the encampment, 38 rifles were confiscated. A medicine man performed the Ghost Dance, dancing in a circle and throwing dust into the air. More guns were taken as they started to search the men, with the young warriors becoming agitated by the search. Tensions were now high among the troops and the Indians. Witnesses from both sides agree on what happened next that provoked the gunfire from the soldiers.

A soldier had confronted Black Coyote, a deaf man that did not speak or understand English, demanding he gives up his rifle. Another Indian tried to explain about Black Coyote not understanding, and when two soldiers grabbed him from behind. In the struggle, his gun was not pointing at anyone, but it discharged, making a loud noise. At this time, the medicine man threw dust into the air, and five Lakota men hiding rifles in their blankets fired at troop K of the 7th Cavalry. After that, all hell broke loose. At first, the exchange was at close range, with half of the Indian men shot before they ever had a chance to fire their weapons. Meanwhile, the Hotchkiss guns fired on the Teepee (Tipi) s, and Indian women and children tried to flee the camp. It is also believed that this act killed many soldiers by friendly fire. The firing continued until nothing was standing in the camp, warriors, older men, women and children, ponies, and dogs, all dead. Young boys that came out of hiding were cut down by the soldiers. Fleeing the camp, many Indians took shelter in a nearby ravine. Those women and children escaping, were followed by soldiers, shot down. Some of the Cavalry chase, killing indiscriminately and discharging into the gorge. Eyewitness reports of the slaughter describe the killing of women and children. Women with babies had been hunted as many as 2 miles from the camp and killed. There was no one in charge of these actions. It is believed the soldiers went berserk, killing indiscriminately. Some of these soldiers were at the Battle of Little Big Horn. Was this the result of reparation against the Indians for the 7th Cavalry that died at Little Big Horn?

An estimated 300 of the 350 at the camp were killed, with the Army having 25 dead and 6 wounded. 20 soldiers received The Medal of Honor for their actions at Wounded Knee.

After the three-day blizzard followed the Wounded Knee Massacre, General Nelson Miles visited the site. To his horror, he could see the 300 dead covered in snow, the women, and children. Civilians were hired to bury the dead in a mass grave. This they did on the hill where the Hotchkiss guns were fired. 50 Indians fleeing Wounded Knee made camp about 15 miles north of Pine Ridge; Company K of the 7th Cavalry was sent to take them to Pine Ridge Indian Reservation. Company K found itself pinned down by the Lakota forces. When the Wounded Knee Massacre occurred, the 9th Cavalry **(Buffalo Soldiers)**, scouting 15 miles north of the Indian Agency at Pine Ridge, came upon and rescued Company K of the 7th, driving off the Indians.

Early morning of **December 30, 1890**, Troops F, I, and K reached the Agency, leaving Troop D behind to guard the supply wagons 3 miles from the Agency. The 50 Lakota warriors attacked the wagons killing a soldier. The soldiers circled the wagons to protect themselves. Indian scouts among the troops refused to go to the fort for help, a Corporal William Wilson volunteered to go. His troops covering him with fire, he raced through the wagons towards the Agency, being chased by the Lakota. He reached the Agency, alarming the soldiers who were able to run off the Lakota. Wilson received the Medal of Honor for his actions. The 9th Cavalry remained at the Pine Ridge Agency through March 1891.

This was now declared the end of the Indian Wars.

Several attempts have been made to rescind the 20 Medals of Honor for the Wounded Knee massacre, calling them tarnished Medals of Honor given to soldiers for genuine acts of courage.

Wounded Knee was listed on the U.S. National Register of Historic Places in 1966.

Metal Detecting Finds

The following are some of the finds discovered metal detecting private properties surrounding a fort and Indian conflicts. This book would not have been possible without the permission to hunt these properties. **All of the artifacts were found by the author and Marcus Waters.**

Borman timed fuse used in cannon balls to explode at a set time in seconds after leaving the cannon.

Friction primers were used firing the cannon. A lanyard was attached to the wire, and pulled through the primer tube filled with gunpowder, creating a spark that ignited the gun powder.

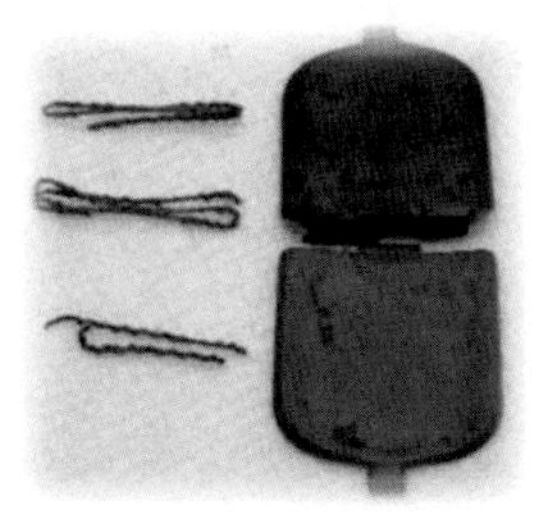

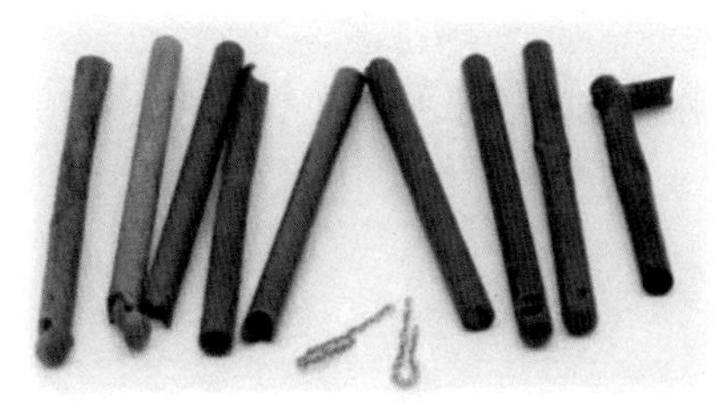

These were used to apply tension to the lines securing tent with stakes.

Examples of the different bullets

Examples of Musket balls

A lead bar from the St Louis Shot Tower Company. This company manufactured musket balls by pouring molten lead through a screen at the top of a tower. When it reached the bottom, it was a perfect sphere and was instantly cooled by the water. They also provided bars of lead that could be cut, and the pieces melted and cast into bullet molds.

Unfired bullets contain gun powder that remains good

Pieces of a Cannon ball that was fired at the Indians.

An example of a bullet dug from hardened clay almost as hard as concrete.

Officers brass epaulet

Copper dividers and a compass used for navigation

Decorative eagle of a dress helmet found by Marcus Waters

Examples of the various Military buttons

Artillery button with the seal of Rhode Island and the "I" for Infantry Eagle button

A variety of the buttons found.

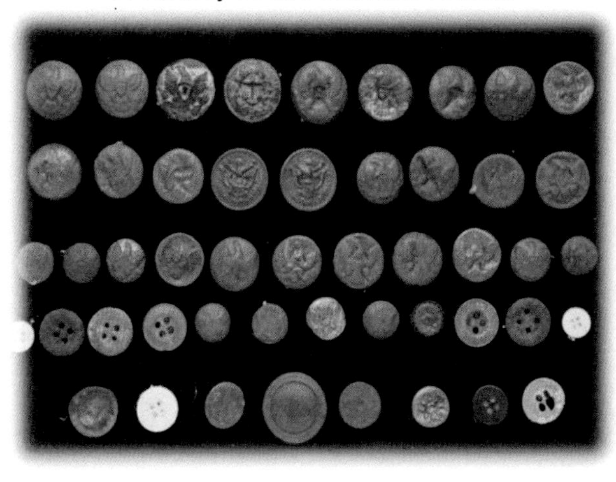

A War Veterans badge, Grand Army of the Republic (GAR) Veterans that served in the Civil War. Found by Marcus Waters

Amunition pouch fastener

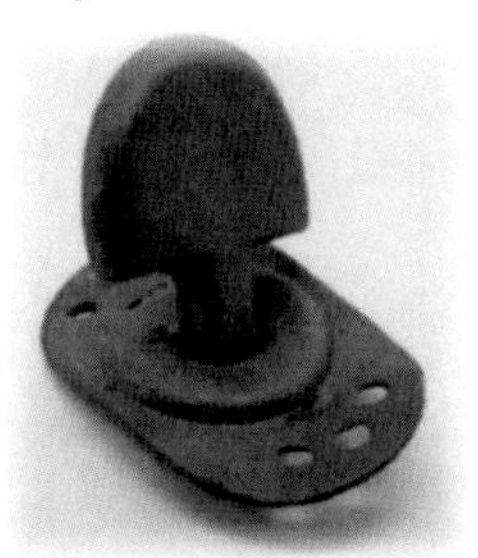

Ladies ring

Ladies 18k gold Broach

Bell **Singer sewing machine tag**

Wood chisel

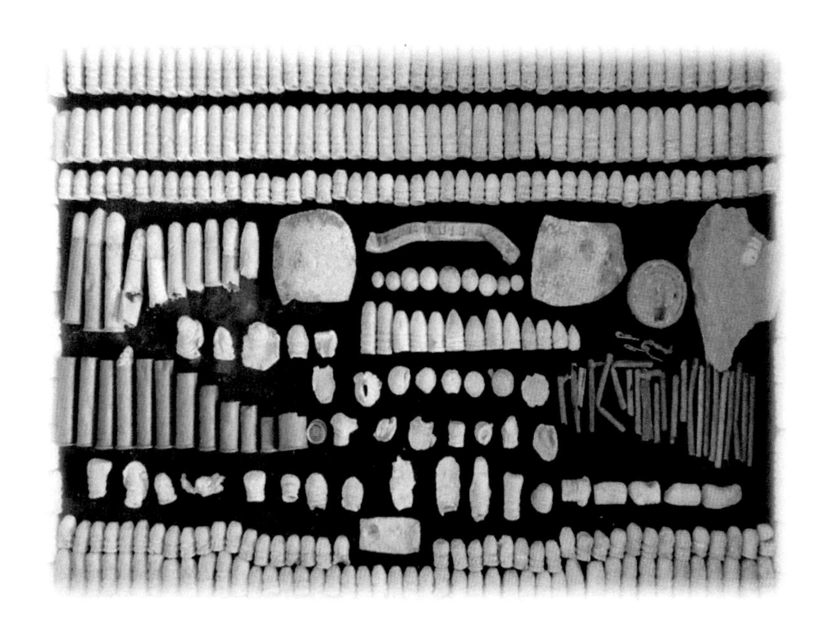

Display cases of artifacts found.

Summary

Throughout history, there have always been injustices. There has always been a progression, but how we move forward determines the justifications. Native Americans were forced onto reservations to farm and live off the government. Losing their nomadic way of life, following the buffalo herds and gold-rich land. Fast forward to the present, some enjoy the wealth generated from casinos, others from oil-rich land, but others live in not-so-illustrious circumstances. Generations have suffered from drinking problems and poverty while living on the reservations.

In the 1868 Fort Laramie Treaty, The Great Sioux reservation covered all of South and North Dakota. This included the Missouri River and the sacred Black Hills, with the rights to follow the buffalo and hunt off the reservation into Wyoming and Montana. Written into the treaty, "no cession of land would be valid unless approved by three-fourths of the adult males." Disregarding this, and due to the discovery of gold, Congress, in 1877, passed an act to remove the sacred Black Hills from the Great Sioux reservation. This was without the required consent of the Sioux. In 1980, in the lawsuit United States v. Sioux Nation of Indians, the US Supreme Court concluded. **"A more ripe and rank case of dishonorable dealings will never, in all probability, be found in our history."**

Of the forts, battlefields, and monuments I visited, Little Big horn had gravestones for Indian warriors and the Indian Memorial. Fort Buford had a few gravesites in the cemetery, and Whitestone Hill had a small plaque on a stone pillar honoring the deaths of Indians killed. Other than Little Big Horn, I have not seen a monument honoring the Indians massacred during these conflicts.

Something extraordinary is happening near Rapid City, South Dakota. A monument is being carved out of a mountain, the Crazy horse monument. So much more prominent than Mount Rushmore, with not a penny of government money. It will be surrounded by a college campus for the Native American youth when complete. A chance to learn a trade and not be dependent on anyone. I visited this site in 2021 and was impressed with the newer technology used to create the monument. GP, laser technology, and diamond saws enabled the removal of five feet of rock from the pointing arm's length in only two weeks.

Tasunke Witko: A monument to Crazy Horse is being created near Rapid City South Dakota

Bibliography

Encyclopedia of Indian Wars by Gregory F. Michno

Whitestone Hill by Clair Jacobson

Whitestone Battlefield by The Whitestone Battlefield Celebration Committee.

The National Parks Service Information from National Parks, battlefields, and monuments visited.

North Dakota State Parks Information from State parks, fort and historic sites visited.

State Historical Society of North Dakota Information from the on-line site concerning, people, battles, and forts of North Dakota.

Wikipedia Information concerning people, battles, and forts of the Indian wars.

Jeffery Banke Photograph of Buffalo

Marcus Waters Metal detecting skills

About the Author

FRED BANKE is a U.S. Navy veteran, FAA-certified aircraft mechanic, and long-time metal detectorist. After graduating from Colorado Aero tech with an A&P license, he enjoyed a successful career in composite repair with FlightSafety International. He served as a consultant to both NASA and the United Space Alliance. Fred's been detecting the Treasure Coast for over a decade, finally "retiring" after years of back-and-forth adventuring.

His latest adventures include traveling to the Dakotas, researching forts and battlefields of the Indian Wars, and metal-detecting private properties to find artifacts of the same. The author's previous book, "The Reale Deal Metal Detecting The Florida Treasure Coast," has been a bestseller in both local Museums.

Made in the USA
Columbia, SC
08 July 2023